STAND BY AND SEE WHAT THE LORD WILL ACCOMPLISH

The Story of One Family Serving the Lord in Nigeria

By Grace J. Farrar

STAND BY
AND SEE
WHAT THE LORD
WILL ACCOMPLISH

Copyright 2002 by Mrs. Grace J. Farrar

Catalog Number C-3035
ISBN 1-56794-247-4

Published by
Star Bible Publications
P O Box 821220
Fort Worth, Texas 76180
800 433 7507   www.starbible.com
E-mail: starbible.pub@juno.com

Contents

Preface and Acknowledgment v

Introduction viii

FIRST YEAR: 1964 -- 1965 3

SECOND YEAR: 1965 -- 1966 81

THIRD YEAR: 1966 -- 1967 131

   Addendum 179

PREFACE and ACKNOWLEDGEMENT

Because You Asked

"Mama, will you, please, hurry up and write your book so we won't have to!" Because you asked:

"<u>I take my pen in hand</u>" ... Or more appropriately, I seat myself at the PC our son David ditched when he upgraded. I flip the "ON" switch then go to the kitchen to adjust bouncing lids on the stove while Word Perfect works its way forward. Returning I can now punch "GC," my husband's designation for my part. With time to spare, I change the clothes from the washer to the dryer before the blank screen appears. This computer and I have a lot in common. At our ages we enjoy a more leisurely pace.

"<u>and being sound of mind</u>" ... A septuagenarian is after all thirty years short of a centenarian, but then I hope to enjoy that age as well.

"<u>I set down for posterity</u>" ... No less than six kids and six grandkids -- as of this date.

"<u>a record of my first tour in Nigeria</u>." Though not intended to be a history of the Nigerian Christian Hospital (some will of necessity be included), nor an exposition on cross-cultural adjustment (I have opinions about that as well), this is simply the story of a Sarah who by faith loved her Lord, her husband, and her children enough to leave her homeland "not knowing where (she) was going."

On my return in 1967, after three years in Nigeria, I found myself answering an endless number of questions about our personal lives there -- "What kind of house did you live in? What did you eat? What did your children do for fun? How did they feel about living in Nigeria? How did you balance being a wife, mother, home-school teacher and missionary?" -- and many more. For all who wanted to know here are my answers -- because you asked.

Thanks, Mom, I Couldn't Have Done It Without You

Henry did the dreams and I did the "drums" (eleven of those 50-gallon steel barrels used for shipping personal effects, to be exact) -- a succinct summary of our pre-Nigeria preparation.

Once there my time was so occupied that I decided I could do double duty by making carbon copies of my letters as a kind of journal. When we were evacuated just before the Biafran War began, the general mood among expatriates was "this will soon blow over." Expecting only a temporary dislocation, I left all those papers behind. How thankful I am for my mother who prized every letter.

Aware that my letters were destined to make the rounds among family and friends, I addressed them ambiguously to "Dear folks" and signed them with my family nickname, "Dit." (I have been told that my first vocal sound was "Dit" and that I was so pleased with this accomplishment my family was almost berserk before I shifted my vocal cords to another syllable.)

I am thankful also to my daughters -- Marty, who took time from her busy family and professional schedules to read the manuscript and make suggestions, and Samantha, who patiently struggled hoping to make me computer literate.

INTRODUCTION

Jim Bill McInteer, serving as preacher for the West End Church of Christ, Nashville, Tennessee, wrote the following article for the church bulletin to introduce our family to the congregation prior to our departure.

WEST END VISITOR
July 10, 1964

The Mission of the church is MISSIONS!

Dr. Henry Farrar, a former member of the surgical staff of the Veterans Administration Hospital in Johnson City, Tennessee, until his resignation June 30th, will preach his last sermons at West End, Sunday, July 12, before leaving with his family for a tour of duty as the first "preaching physician" sent by the West End church to Nigeria.

Dr. Farrar with his wife and five children will leave Monday, July 13th, for Nigeria.

Dr. Farrar, a native of Nashville, attended Harding College, Searcy, Arkansas; received his B.S. and M. A. degrees from the University of Tennessee. In 1947 and 1949 while a student at U.T., he was a member of the Phi Kappa Phi. His M.D. degree was awarded by the School of Medicine, University of Tennessee, Memphis, March '54, receiving the Verstandig award for his class on graduation. Dr. Farrar interned at Tampa Municipal Hospital, Tampa, Florida. His surgical residency was at Harlan, Kentucky Memorial Hospital 1957-60 and City Memorial Hospital, Winston-Salem, North Carolina 1960-62. From 1962 until his resignation he served on the surgical staff of the V.A. Hospital in Johnson City, Tennessee and is certified as a Diplomate of the American Board of Surgery.

Dr. Farrar's wife, Grace, is a registered nurse from Bethesda Hospital, Cincinnati, Ohio, having made the highest grade on the Ohio

State Board of Nursing. She graduated from Harding College with the B.S. degree in 1948 also being selected for "Who's Who in American Colleges and Universities."

Paul (11), Martha (9), David (7), Hank (5), and Lee (3) are the children of Dr. Farrar. His mother is Mrs. Henry Farrar, Sr., of Nashville and his brother, George Farrar, is a member of the West End church.

Last year, with Jack Sinclair, one of the West End's elders, a tour of inspection was made in Nigeria. Already extensive medical equipment and supplies have been sent to Nigeria. The area of Dr. Farrar's service will be Eastern Ngwa, Nigeria; temporarily on arrival he may work two months at Port Harcourt.

" Fifty-two million people live in Nigeria -- their medical needs are exceeded only by their spiritual needs. It is our hope to have a part in bringing the light of truth to dispel spiritual darkness and the healing arts of medicine to relieve the suffering of humanity even as did the Great Physician himself," voiced Dr. Farrar.

The West End church will support Dr. Farrar as a "preaching physician" and provide the necessary work fund.

Correction: Obviously it was Henry who reported the children's ages. In July 1964, Paul was 11, Marty was 10, David was 8, Hank was 6, and Lee would celebrate his 4th birthday that month.

The University of Tennessee, College of Medicine, Charles C. Verstandig Award referred to was awarded to the graduate who had overcome the most obstacles and voted most deserving of the degree by fellow classmates and the faculty. The honor is one of the highest given by the college and included a physician's handbag.

Our First Year
1964 - 1965

The Farrars arriving in Port Harcourt, Nigeria. In the front are David, Paul, Marty & Hank. In the back are Henry & Grace. Lee apparently ran ahead. (Photo by John Beckloff) (July, 1964)

Missionary Co-workers

(l-r) Nancy Petty, Henry Farrar & Iris Hays. (Henry put his arm behind him to hide his cast). (1965)

Dr. John & Donna Morgan wearing farewell Nigerian gifts. (1965)

Ruth, Dayton, Dita & Tonya Keesee (1965)

Charla, Douglas, Shauna, Tami & Cindi Lawyer (1966)

Barbara, Windle, Alicejoy & Paul Kee (1967)

Mary Lou, Clifford, Patti Nell, Bill & Barton Curry at Onich Ngwa BTC (1963)

(l-r) Davey, Myra, Becky, Brian Bris & David Underwood (1965)

Patti, Rees, Billy, Becki, David & Sara Jo Bryant (1967)

In flight
July 25, 1964

Dear folks,

"Sitting on top of the clouds," as Lee puts it, I have a moment to highlight our seven days in New York and five in London.

We left Nashville at 10 a.m. on the 13th as scheduled expecting to be met by Dwain Evans of the Exodus Bay Shore group at LaGuardia about 4 p.m. From Philadelphia on, the word "turbulence" was redefined for us. After circling LaGuardia for two hours, or more, because of the rain and fog, Marty was grabbing for the "urp bag" while Lee was laughing at all the "tickle bumps" -- "because they tickle my tummy," he explained.

Finally the word came to land in Newark, N.J., and from there we were bussed back to New York. It was dark, more nearly 8 p.m., when we finally arrived. To our amazement there stood Dwain faithfully waiting to take us home with him.

The next day we rented a car and moved into a fishing cabin he had reserved for us on Long Island. Our plan was to spend several days at the New York World's Fair. My preparation for the Fair had included five red baseball caps for quick counts topside and an ID luggage tag fastened to each kid's belt in case one strayed.

The crowds exceeded our expectations. I ran mental counts -- 1-2-3-4-5-- so often throughout every day that I became scarcely aware of it. Whenever the count suddenly stopped at 4, I screamed, "STOP!" and everyone froze till we backtracked to find number 5.

Leaving the Illinois building, I counted, "1-2-3-4--STOP!"

The missing person was Lee. When we found him, he had already calmly shown his tag to the guard explaining, "This is who I am." We interrupted the guard just as he was taking Lee to get an ice cream cone. Lee will never forgive such bad timing.

On Sunday we worshipped with the Exodus group, meeting in their new building for the first time. That evening we were asked to stand before the congregation while they sang "Speed Away" and had a prayer for us. Even recalling that song now brings chill bumps of emotion.

London! The storybook town of my childhood where a Dick Whittington can make it to the top and a pussy cat visits the queen! But the guides told other stories. All that glamour was washed away by history, as I heard again and again how "on this very spot" some royalty had been hanged or beheaded.

Philip Slate, the American missionary serving at Wembly, had made reservations for us at the Academy Hotel convenient to the British Museum and the School for Tropical Medicine. The hotel was in one of those long rows of houses joined together with front doors flush with the sidewalk -- the low-cost, share-the-bath, bed & breakfast sort that students frequent. In fact the breakfasts were so huge they could hold us till evening with only a noon snack -- in spite of the British fancy for half-cooked eggs, limp bacon and toast cooled on special racks.

We soon learned why the British were never known for their culinary skills. "Wimpy burgers" were an instant hit, but other familiar sounding items were sometimes surprises. Who could have guessed that London's "Kentucky pancake" would come swimming in a tomato sauce -- certainly no one from the Bluegrass State.

The kids had such a great time it would be hard to say what was most memorable for them. Not to be discounted were the rides atop double decker buses and, with the new long hair styles, the fun of guessing who was a "him" and who was a "her" or spotting a "Beatle" on every corner.

Perhaps best was the changing of the guards at Buckingham Palace. Drawing on his own personal experience, Lee's sense of awe was not quite the same as for Christopher Robin. Lee kept asking how they got so dirty they had to be changed.

Lee says, "Tell Grandpa, `Yes'."

Love,
Dit

(Lee and his Grandpa Johnson had a thing going between the two of them. If one said, "Yes," the other would immediately answer, "No," or vice versa. No other discussion was needed.)

July 26, 1964

The Nigerian Airway's Fokker burst through the low-lying clouds of rainy season. Sprawling below me was a vast expanse of what resembled upside-down green feather dusters interspersed with the broad leafed fingers of banana and plantain trees. The voice of an Egyptian pilot was announcing our arrival into Port Harcourt Airport.

As the wheels struck the tarmac, the windows steamed over. I had already encountered the Nigerian elements face to face passing through Lagos, and the most vivid description I had heard came from an expatriate who had said he felt as if he had been suddenly wrapped in a hot, wet blanket.

I made my split-second kid-check, -- 1-2-3-4-5 -- all here! Pausing at the doorway to size up the precariously steep stair to the ground and shifting my carry-on overload for a firmer grip, I glanced at the waiting crowd. It was not hard to spot our welcoming party amid all the upturned Nigerian faces.

There were Bill and Mary Lou Curry, friends since Harding days. At the World's Fair we had unexpectedly met them and their three preschoolers -- Barton, Clifford, and Patti Nell -- all of us en route to Nigeria.

Also waiting for us were Doug and Charla Lawyer, Harding contemporaries. Hadn't Doug's sense of humor been the stuff of which college legends are made! What an asset to the mission field! And what a joy to know that their three -- Shauna, Tami, and Cindi -- were the ages of our own! Both families were now on a second tour at the Onicha Ngwa Bible Training College where we would be living.

We were introduced for the first time to other families who were to become very important in our lives. John and Dottie Beckloff, originally from Oklahoma, were now on a second tour living at Ikot Usen, more than an hour's drive from Onicha Ngwa. The Beckloff's four -- John, Dean, Mark, and Nancy -- were nearly the same ages as our own and would mean more friends for ours.

Also greeting us were the families working with the Bible College at Ukpom -- Joe and Dorothy Cross from Odessa, Texas, with their two -- Scotty and Melody, and the Otoyos -- Eno, Lavera and their daughter. A native of Oyubia, a village near Oron, Eno had married Lavera, a Texan, while studying in the States.

I had already learned that peace of mind in air travel meant bidding all baggage good-by when you check it in. If it shows up when and where you do, you can rejoice and be glad; if not, it will be no more than expected. Everything had arrived!

In the airport lounge Charla Lawyer, always sensitive to the needs of others, unpacked the lunch she had prepared for us -- sandwiches, drinks, and cookies. Truly a welcome feast! It was now past noon, but having envisioned an invisible world of creepy, crawly, unnamables, our boldest venture in the Lagos airport had been to have a bottled drink.

My practical education for living in the tropics began immediately. A Detol-treated washcloth substituted for a washbasin. Airport restrooms were BYOSP (bring your own soap and paper). A quick napkin swipe around the top of the drink bottle removed the rust. In this high humidity rust and molds are the norm.

Like a multi-screen National Geographic movie, scenes of Nigerian life flashed by all sides of our car for the next fifty miles to Onicha Ngwa. Head balancing acts included everything from an umbrella or a bottle to a table or a bed frame. A bicycle was obviously the family car. With papa at the pedals, mama often rode sidesaddle behind balancing a baby on her back or a headpan of produce, sometimes both. More little ones often perched on the handlebars or frame. It occurred to me that our children were now seeing all the rules of bicycle safety so carefully drilled into them as Scouts being flagrantly violated without disastrous results.

Without air-conditioning the car windows were down, and hawkers were quick to take advantage of any "go-slow" (traffic slowdown). Black faces, openly curious, peered inside the car. Loaves of bread and rolls of toilet paper were dangled before our eyes with pleas to purchase. Headpans of bananas, oranges, greens, and produce of every kind were brought down to eye level. Even bras strung on long shoulder poles were waved enticingly. These roadside entrepreneurs, mostly children, appeared to have every possible saleable item.

I feared for their lives as they darted in and out dodging the rolling traffic. Sunday was not a market day, but even so this had to be the land of the ultimate in free enterprise. I couldn't imagine communism ever getting a foothold in Nigeria.

Our oldest son Paul, one who by natural inclination did not speak unless spoken to, rode with the Otoyos to Onicha Ngwa. Initiating conversation, Lavera told me later she had asked Paul, "What is you first impression of Nigeria?" And he had answered, "I never saw so many black people in my life." Laughing Lavera, also black, had replied, "Paul, when I first came, that was exactly what I thought too."

On our arrival at the Bible Training College, we were greeted by a huge white welcome banner stretched high across the dirt road. On the right side of the road were the classrooms and dormitories for the Bible College on land sloping to a stream behind. On a hill to the left overlooking the school were the houses for the missionary families. We were taken immediately to the large central house that was to be our home. Looking out our front door toward the school, we could see the Lawyers' house to our right and the Currys' to our left.

Awaiting our arrival were more than three hundred local citizens, mostly members of the churches and village officials, crowded in and around the main classroom designed for about thirty Bible students and literally hanging out the outer walls which were about waist high to allow for cross-ventilation. Henry wanted to dash down immediately and greet everyone, but Doug, more experienced with travel in the tropics, insisted that we first have a cold drink and rest for an hour. He assured us that the waiting crowd would be very happy singing while we rested. And to our amazement they were. The singing -- strange words to familiar tunes -- was still lusty when we all went downhill to the school. Emotions were high as the voices of those who had waited long for a doctor joined that of the doctor who had waited long to realize his life's dreams.

For the next two hours my mind swirled as strange faces, strange names, strange sounds, and strange smells all enmeshed in a jet-lag haze. Group after group greeted us with welcoming speeches, songs, and "dashes" (gifts) while the whole program was translated through three languages -- Ibo, Efik, and English. At our feet lay a huge array of tropical produce -- bananas, oranges, pineapple, pawpaws, yams, coconuts, and foods I'd never before seen or heard of. There were eggs, live chickens, and even an unwilling goat. I will never forget one little lady presenting Henry with an offering of eggs and adding, "I would gladly cook them for you, but your wife will know best how you like to eat them."

That Sunday evening the sermon was delivered by J. O. Akandu, the Nigerian headmaster of the Bible school. Oxford English spoken with an African intonation was yet another foreign language to me. I understood only one word of the entire sermon -- "salt." Obviously the text was Matthew 5:13.

When the generator providing the lights and fans went off that night at 10:00, I crawled under a mosquito net for the first time. A chorus of insects and frogs outside my window and the sounds of distant drums blended into a soothing lullaby. We had finally arrived and all was well.

The "Farrar House"

The "Farrar House" incorporated the best input from the Nicks, Lawyers, and Bryants who had lived in Nigeria for many years. Geographically, the area was only slightly more then five degrees north of the Equator. The absence of cooling electricity soon proved to them the basic principles in designing a tropical home -- allow for plenty of cross-ventilation to catch the prevailing breeze from the ocean and shut out as much of the hot western sun as possible.

When the first resident missionaries for the churches of Christ, Howard Horton and Jimmy Johnson with their families, arrived in 1952 they lived in mud houses with palm thatch roofs. Two years later when construction began for the Ukpom Bible College, houses of landcrete blocks (made from the soil mixed with cement) were built for the missionaries. Construction did not keep up with the number of families arriving. Families might share the same house until another could be built -- sometimes for as long as a year.

In 1958 J.W. Nicks and James Finney moved with their families from Ukpom to Iboland to open the Bible Training College (BTC) at Onicha Ngwa, and each built a landcrete house on the campus with quarters for any workers who wanted to take advantage of the convenience. When we arrived, the "Nicks House" was occupied by the Lawyers and Currys lived in the "Finney House."

When planning for a third house, the missionaries decided to make it large enough for more than one family should the need arise again. Then the Farrars came with a family large enough for two.

While the Proctor Street church of Port Arthur, Texas, sponsored the BTC, missionary families were responsible for raising their own house funds and work funds. We were the thankful to have been relieved of that burden. The Lawyers, who had helped raise money for the construction of the third house, had been living in it. Even though they lacked another year completing their second tour, they graciously moved into the smaller "Nicks House," that had recently been vacated by the return of Jim Massey and his family. The "Lawyer House" became the "Farrar House."

Individually hand-molded, sun dried blocks formed the walls. The floor was overlain with a red Colorcrete that took on a high gloss with an application of Red Mansion floor wax hand-rubbed with a halved coconut husk. Some of the windows were the casement type cranking outward and others were of louvered glass. The biggest expense was the galvanized ("zinc") roofing. The house had two sections --a family area and a kitchen/utility area all under one roof.

A screened front porch led into a large living room area with an adjoining dining area. Three bedrooms were so spacious that the mosquito nets, hung from the ceiling, covered two beds and left room for one to walk around inside the nets. A fourth smaller room had been planned as a schoolroom, but when it became Paul's room, one of the children remarked, "It's all he needs -- just space for a bed and a book."

Henry was delighted to have an office with a separate entrance off the front porch for visitors. With the screened porch on one side and a screened play porch on the other it was cooled by the ocean breeze. A bathroom, and a walk-in storage closet completed the family living section.

A wall separating the kitchen/utility area minimized the heat and noise. With bottled gas for cooking now available, ours was the first missionary house built with an indoor kitchen. (The separate kitchens for wood fires of the earlier houses were later connected to their living areas by breezeways.)

Our back door opened into a hallway leading to the kitchen on the left and to storage and laundry rooms on the right. Closets and shelves were all open for air circulation to prevent molds and mildew.

Utilities included a gasoline ("petrol") generator for electricity and an abundant water supply from the stream at the foot of the hill beyond the school in dry season or off the roof during rainy season. The 50 gallon steel barrels ("drums") used for shipping personal belongings, mounted high at the top of concrete steps, served as reservoirs outside the kitchen and bathroom.

Doug Lawyer, overseeing the BTC, had assigned the students the job of keeping the stream cleaned so that the water would be always moving, never stagnant. Though our area of Nigeria did not have such water borne diseases as schistosomiasis, most American families added a small amount of Detol, a disinfectant, to their bath water. Cooking and drinking water was boiled and filtered.

Our kerosene refrigerator ("fridge") was very efficient. We searched Aba to replace the British oven, not even large enough for my cookie sheets, and found one American gas stove with an oven so big the cook could bake a week's supply of bread at one time and conserve the expensive bottled gas. A petrol wringer type washing machine had replaced hand washing.

We even had an intercom between houses. The Lawyers lived so near that our kids thought it was hilarious when they were on the play porch to see and hear Doug calling from his office to Henry's.

With the basic furniture already supplied, we could immediately settle in while we planned for more furniture and decorated the house in our own personal style. One of my first requests was for a planter on the front porch high enough for the greenery to show through the living room window. When it was completed, I proudly filled it with caladium, sansevieria, and other tropical plants with colorful, striking foliage that I had found in the bush. As I stood back admiring my work, I heard my astonished steward say, "You think those things are beautiful! We pull them up and throw them out of our gardens!"

While friends at home were probably envisioning us in mud huts, we were enjoying the most spacious house we'd ever lived in, but one blessed with its own bugs -- organic and inorganic.

It seemed that plumbs and squares had not yet reached the Nigerian toolbox. As Patti Bryant noted, "You won't find a square corner anywhere."

Week One

I will always be grateful to every pioneer missionary who rolled a stone from my path. Cross-cultural adjustment had not yet been well defined, but I knew before going to Nigeria that daily living would require a lot of knowledge not found in the books. How grateful I was, especially during those first few days, for two very practical on-the-spot guides, Charla Lawyer and Mary Lou Curry.

After having stocked our pantry with the food basics and things she thought we would want to know were available, Charla had explained, "These are the things our family enjoys, but if you do not like any I will be happy to buy them back." For the first few days we were invited to have meals with the other families, giving us a chance to recover from jet-lag and to ask a million questions.

And ask I did! I had already determined to remember that I was a guest who had been invited by strangers into their homeland, and I would behave as I would want my guests to behave. I would keep my eyes, ears, and mind wide open for all I could learn, and my mouth shut -- except for the questions.

Charla had arranged for the usual household helpers -- cook, steward, yardmen, and a washerman. She explained, "These are Christian men that we think will do well, but if you are not pleased with any, you are free to dismiss them and hire anyone you choose." I had no idea what I needed, much less what I might want.

Unaccustomed to servants, I felt uncomfortable with the idea until I learned how valuable the job was to them and their families. Also our servants had servants -- usually a relative, or some "small boy," who did such things as carry their wood and water in return for food, lodging and perhaps school fees. I saw their service as replacing the electrical servants I had enjoyed in America and performing the tasks for which I had no time.

Even among the workers there seemed to be a kind of hierarchy -- the indoor servants and the outdoor servants. At the top was the cook, Tom Ibe, a man of rare ability and years of experience cooking for Europeans. I found out he could prepare any recipe given him. He turned out glazed yeast doughnuts that rivaled Krispy Kreme, great pizzas, and pastries you could flake with a fork piled high with artistic meringue. Although he never tasted our food, he knew when things looked and smelled right. Always careful and clean, he would never think of mixing meat loaf or cookie dough with his hands the way I did.

I was the one with the problem. Writing menus for the day so he could plan his work was so different from my usual what's-in-the-refrigerator approach to meals. Nor was it any easier composing recipes for my dash-of-this-or-that dishes. The only goofs he made were the results of my Americanisms, such as adding sugar to the milk because I had written "sweet milk" or the time he cooked beet tops in an orange sauce because I had written "beets" and not specified the British term "beet root."

My steward, Monday John Akpakpan, was an honor student at the BTC and worked in the afternoons after his morning classes. His responsibilities were chiefly cleaning the house, boiling our water, washing dishes, and helping the cook.

Emanuel Ekpendu and Peter Enemannah were our two yardmen who carried water, cut the grass with a "machet" (machete), washed the car, and did any other outside work needed. The washerman, John Ahukannah, came two or three times a week.

Each had his own "specialty." The yardman collected fire wood and carried wash water to fill a big black pot for John to heat. If the petrol operated machine refused to go, (which was frequent) John, not a mechanic, knew only how to clean the spark plug. If that did not help, the washing was done by hand until Peter, the Ukpom mechanic, could come.

The clothes pressing iron was a very ingenious appliance with a hollow cavity for hot charcoal. When I picked it up, I decided that the weight alone was enough to flatten any wrinkles. Nigerians laundrymen liked to starch the buttoned style shirts heavily, then put a military crease across the back. However I was never given to starching and pressing. Since we did not live in an area infested with the tumbu flies that deposit eggs on clothes hung outside to dry (which hatch on the skin unless killed by ironing with the larvae causing boils) and since having hot charcoal meant first collecting the wood and making the charcoal, both John and I was happy to dispense with the ironing.

The lack of familiarity with my surroundings made me approach every aspect very cautiously. I wanted to help Tom because our family was larger than the Masseys he had been cooking for, but I felt like a stranger in my own kitchen. I decided to begin with Jello ("jelly," the British say). Anyone can do that, or so I thought. My "jelly" refused to jell. How could I possibly fail at Jello? And in the presence of a professional cook! Later Charla explained that the British measuring cup has 2 more ounces than the American one. For American recipes, I should use American measurements.

Mary Lou told me, "Take a lot of photos the first six weeks because after that things will begin to seem natural." Even so I was warned that you can't go wildly swinging your camera about. Some Nigerians would ask you to take their picture if they saw your camera, and even ask for a print. Others might demand money or even be angry. One expatriate, not a missionary, had had the film yanked from his camera for taking a nude bathing scene in a roadside stream. "Photogenic Nigerian culture," he thought, but the one who confiscated his film said, " I won't let you take our nudity back to America and laugh at us." Would I appreciate someone entering my bathroom for a tub shot? Caution and consideration were the watchwords.

And then there was the language barrier. I spoke English. The British spoke English. The Nigerians spoke English. But none of us sounded alike. In fact, I could scarcely understand the other two.

A British colony before 1960 composed of approximately 250 ethnic groups each with its own tribal tongue, Nigeria had made English the official language when it became independent -- British English, that is. The British meaning for very familiar words could be quite different from the American.

We were told that all white people in Nigeria were referred to as "Europeans" regardless of their origin. As terms of respect I would be called "Madam" and Henry would be "Master." "Madam" carried a different connotation for me -- and it was not one of respect. But I could handle it, if that was what they wanted. Henry, on the other hand, couldn't tolerate "Master." It made him feel like a slave driver, he said. I don't think they ever understood his insistence on "Doctor," especially since British surgeons consider "Doctor" demeaning to their specialty and are called "Mister" as the proper title for their status.

Mary Lou had suggested, "Think of your time here as a long camp-out and you won't mind the primitiveness as much." Nothing appealed to me more. Hadn't I grown up in the make-it-do, make-it-last days of the Depression. I was happy to be back to basics.

During the first week, the Lawyers hosted a welcoming dinner party for us and invited all the missionary families including those from Ukpom and Ikot Usen. Charla even had a chocolate cake with four candles to celebrate Lee's birthday. She had explained beforehand that they enjoyed making the most of every special occasion. As a gracious hostess, she certainly knew how.

Part of that specialness, she had said, was the opportunity to dress up. For me, make-up fell under the heading of "social artificialities." Applying it at home, had always prompted my kids to ask, "Where are you going?" In America, make-up served as my answer to an inevitable question (spoken or unspoken) put to a mother of five, "No, the kids are not getting me down." In Africa just the fact of my having five children made its own statement as to my worth and emotional well-being, and aging itself was respected. It came as a surprise to me that what I had thought I could so happily leave behind would be important here. Did it serve as a link to the home culture?

Oh well, now where had I put that lipstick?

August 3, 1964

Dear folks,

Every day is full of surprises, but the biggest came yesterday when Paul awoke with every classical symptom of acute appendicitis. As he heaved, Tom, our cook, stood by sadly muttering, "Ndo, ndo (Ibo for sorry)." Henry whisked Paul off to the Shell Oil Hospital at Port Harcourt for an emergency appendectomy by one of their surgeons. Then he had to fly to Lagos for the day to straighten out a confusion about the visa quota, so he sent Friday, the driver, back to get me to stay with Paul. We're so thankful to have emergency medical care when we need it. The poor Nigerians don't -- and that's why we are here.

Tomorrow we hope to pick up our new 404 Peugot station wagon with a luggage rack. After careful research, Henry decided that this was the best car for our family's size as well as the most durable and economical. It's the "motor" (local term for car) most taxis use, and they really take a beating on these roads.

Our plans are still indefinite. Backdoor practice is illegal. Henry insists that any clinic should be provided by the community. Missionary experience has shown that people do not appreciate what is given freely as much as if it had cost them something. Though local officials have welcomed us profusely with daily dashes and visits, they have yet to produce any funds. We would like to settle here at Onicha Ngwa because of the Bible College and the American families, but other places are begging for us and have funds waiting. It seems to be a kind of cat-and-mouse game, each waiting for the other to make a move.

This bargaining spirit about everything is new to us -- frustrating and confusing. Henry would be the first to admit that patience was never his forte, and he seems to have found the best place to develop the virtue. In fact one co-worker kidded Henry that he was so restless to begin practice he had to operate on his own son.

Otherwise we are all doing great. Our household helpers are all clean, capable, Christian -- and affordable. Their salaries total about $45/mo. Tom has ten children of his own and loves ours. The feeling is mutual. While I was at the hospital with Paul, he not only took good care of the others he even got the younger ones to nap -- something

I've not been able to do. They really enjoy their new playmates, a large lawn with swings, a sandbox, and even a playhouse.

We sleep under nets, spray the house, rub on repellent, and take antimalarials. As for the mosquitos, I'm told "you never see the one that gets you." The anopheles mosquito that carries malaria is very small, but at every bug bite Lee howls that a "laria pesquito" got him.

While other families were feeding us the first week, the dashes accumulated. Charla suggested, "You have all the ingredients. Ask Tom to make ground nut stew (chicken cooked in a sauce of peanut butter with chopped fruits as condiments)." Peanuts are called "ground nuts" here, maybe because they grow in the ground. It was the first meal Tom cooked for our family, and the children went wild, asking if they could have it every day.

Lee, especially, has been fascinated by the "local color." He watched a small boy balancing a large can of water on his head with such admiration that the boy, conscious of being the center of attention, put his hands down to his side and marched on straight as a rod balancing the can perfectly. Lee turned to me wistfully, "I wish I had a brown face, so I could carry things on my head."

This is rainy season. Showers come quickly, and we dry off quickly when the sun comes out. People walk around in the rain like ducks -- even hang out the clothes in the rain. Humidity is so high the clothes never really dry anyway. We've learned to sleep on clammy sheets. Days are muggy and nights cool enough for the kids' flannel pajamas.

Love,
Dit

August 10, 1964

Dear folks,

Saturday (Aug. 8) was a big day for everyone. First Henry went to the Shell Compound to check Paul out of the hospital. Families from both Bible schools met at the Port Harcourt airport to welcome Rees and Patti Bryant and their family arriving for their third tour. When the plane landed, only Patti and the younger three got off.

Just 15 minutes before their departure time in Lagos, Sara Jo, the 9-year-old Marty has been waiting for, had caught her finger in a door and cut it so badly that Rees had to find a doctor to sew it up. The two spent the night at the SIM (Sudan Interior Mission) rest house and came the next day. Some opportunist took advantage of the confusion to make Rees' new movie camera his own.

Patti and I had been co-teachers for the pre-school Bible class at the College Church in Searcy, Arkansas, when she was in high school, and I had met Rees at their wedding. Though many factors had entered into Henry's decision to go to Nigeria, the most decisive had probably been Patti's persuasive power with a pen. She wrote describing the pitiful medical needs, told how Bible teachers could not get their work done for transporting those desperately ill to hospitals, the nearest eleven miles, and ended with the poignant plea, "Where are our Christian doctors?"

Three days ago Henry pulled a muscle in his right knee while playing tennis with Doug. (Doug has made a great tennis court on the BTC campus.) At the airport someone commented on how much Paul looked like Henry -- "even walks like him." I looked at them -- Henry listing to the right favoring his knee and Paul listing to the right favoring his side. "That's right!" I had to agree.

Almost every day another delegation arrives with dashes. Once it was a live lamb. I had just been to the "cold store" (British for a frozen foods shop) and my freezer space is small, so I led the lamb by his vine rope to the yardman and asked that he be tied to the clothesline.

At five the next morning the lamb was bleating so hard, Henry shook me awake with, " You have to go see about that animal!"

When the lamb saw me, he made a lunge that broke the rope and headed for the bush. Monday, my steward, came running out of his quarters saying, "I'll catch him for you, Madam." Only twenty-two and very agile, he gave the lamb a merry chase then lost him to the dense bush. Such an animal is a big gift here. I really regretted losing him, if only for the sake of those who had given him.

The next morning both Tom and Monday came to work out of breath proudly leading the lamb. Before the lamb could make another escape, Tom butchered him and made a great barbecue sauce. Stepping into the kitchen, I was horrified to see the bloody head on the counter -- wide glassy eyes fixed on me.

"What do you plan to do with THAT?" I demanded.

"Put it in the soup pot." Tom replied calmly.

"Not my soup! Keep it for your own."

Tom was so happy he offered to share it with the others who'd helped in the capture.

Campus personnel has been changing. Bill Curry and Dayton Keesee with their families have been sharing a house on the BTC campus which they vacated for the Bryants. They have moved to Enugu, capital city for the Eastern Region, where they hope to begin another Bible school.

Three student preachers from Fort Worth Christian College -- John, Roger, and Ed -- have arrived to work for six months. They're staying in the servant quarters behind Bryants' house, since Bryants' workers live in the village, and having meals with the families. They had scarcely slept for the two days en route, but when I asked one if he would like to nap, he answered, "I came to work, not nap." He'll learn.

Love,
Dit

August 16, 1964

Dear folks,

Sunday is a good day for me to write. The men go on preaching appointments in the mornings, sometimes all day, Then we all meet in the school building for an evening service in English. Paul went with his dad while I had a Bible class for the other school age children on campus. How could I teach the Nigerian children about the Bible and neglect our own?

Paul came home saying he got more attention than the sermon. The area was so remote that the people had never seen a white child before. Charla says that's why she doesn't take her children on preaching trips. The Nigerians love children, and she felt they might be a distraction.

Last week I had my first experience lecturing through an interpreter. The Ukpom Bible College has an annual ladies lectureship while the preaching students are on "holiday" (vacation). Then the school's facilities and Bible teachers are available for the women. Why are all the interpreters men? Is it because they have no educated Efik woman who understands English or because this is such a male-dominated society?

I was asked to speak on health issues. Since most of the women have never attended school, I studied local school hygiene textbooks for practical suggestions. The other missionaries told me later that the simple rules I gave -- covering food from flies, washing hands before handling food, not drinking the same stream water you bathe in without first letting the dirt settle then boiling or sun-sterilizing it, etc.-- were news to many; but I'd have to march them by a microscope if I expected them to believe in germs. With no word in their language for germs, the interpreter resorted to the English. I couldn't help wondering what they must have been picturing. No wonder he used so many words to say so little.

The women's lectureship is a big social event. The women trek or cycle, some as far as 30 miles, with their mats, pots, and food, often carrying little ones on their backs. They spread their sleeping mats on the dorm floors, set up their cooking pots in the yard, beat out their dirty clothes with sticks, and spread them on the grass to dry -- all the time singing as they worked and on into the night.

Their basic menu consists of cassava tuber (manioc) processed into "gari," or yam (not our sweet potato) beaten to develop the gluten, which is then rolled into a ball about the size of a large marble using one hand. With the press of a thumb, the ball forms a kind of spoon to dip into a soup pot. The nutrition is in the soup. The soup usually has fresh greens, tomatoes, onions, pounded okra to make it slimy, very hot peppers and very yellow, acrid-smelling palm oil for seasoning. Some kind of meat or dried fish is added, if they can afford it. Whatever hangs onto the gari ball as it is lifted out of the soup is swallowed all in one gulp -- no chewing.

(The first time I saw a yardman eating his lunch, fingers dripping with slimy yellow greens, I thought I would lose mine. Oh, well, "delicious" is all in the tongue of the eater.)

I had written out my talk word for word in case speaking through an interpreter threw me. It didn't. I had lots of thinking time while he interpreted into Efik. But I missed the audience contact. I felt as if I were speaking only to the interpreter, and who knows what he was saying to them!

Henry finally performed his first surgery here. One of the "watch nights" (night security) had had a tooth abscess so long it had made a hole draining to the outside of his jaw. Not having dental tools, was no problem. The tooth was so loose Henry lifted it with pliers, packed the cavity with sulfa, and then gave him more sulfa to follow up. The man has been very happy with his cure.

The women I see riding a bicycle side saddle behind the men seem to manage easily all kinds of loads at the same time, so I gave it a try. John Beckloff took me side saddle on a bicycle tour of the Ukpom campus. When he stopped, I was so dizzy I had to lie down. That kind of transportation is not for me!

One of the Beckloff boys asked a worker, "Why do you carry everything on your head?" The astonished reply was, "How else would you carry it?"

Love,
Dit

August 26, 1964

Dear folks,

Our drums with "personal effects" were scheduled to arrive on the African Moon Aug. 10, but as Rees says, "The African Moon rises slowly."

We had word that they had arrived in Port Harcourt more than a week ago, but because of a dock strike the boat went on to the next port which happened to be Ghana. There the drums were unloaded and are being returned by "lorry." (A "truck" here is one of the two-wheeled carts we see people pulling around the streets of Aba.)

In the meantime I bought a lot of cloth in the Aba market and have kept my foot treadle sewing machine whirring making sheets, pillow cases, curtains, and bedspreads -- even cloth napkins. The paper napkins are too "dear" (expensive).

I'm so glad I brought a large quantity of thread with me. It's hard to find a good quality thread in the market. If I want thread, I've learned to ask for "cotton." What do I ask for if I want cotton? That's "cotton wool." My vocabulary grows daily.

Henry's hopes for a clinic are presently at a stand-still. The president of the local council, who had promised his financial support in a written letter, now appears to want the clinic for his own profit and power. The local people are trying to raise the money on their own and by-pass the politicians.

Henry is hopeful. They are so very poor, but they are also very numerous. If they can raise three thousand Nigerian pounds (a pound is about $3), the government says it will grant the remainder. Until then Henry has been working at other hospitals in the area and is busy teaching in the school and preaching.

Torrential downpours with clouds shielding the sun keep the weather cooler than I had expected. I know now what the Bible meant by "the heavens opened up." Everyone tells me, "Just wait till dry season if you really want to see tropical heat."

Nigeria is teeming with wildlife, mostly insects. The children, especially David, have been excited over so many kinds of bugs, birds, and lizards. Note: I did not say snakes. So far I have not seen one. There are so many people that if a snake still remains, I'm sure he's afraid to stick his head out for fear of being "chopped" (eaten).

Lizards ("geckos" David would inform me) are everywhere and happy to share their house with me nodding their red heads at me as I pass. After all, they were here before me. I don't really relish lizard eggs hatching in my lingerie, but I console myself thinking about all the mosquitoes they must be devouring.

Whoever thought magpies were the ultimate avian noise makers has never had a colony of weaver birds outside his bedroom window, especially energetic at dawn and dusk. They strip the palm fronds to weave intricate nests resembling baby booties and soon leave nothing but nests hanging onto bare stems. A long-tailed bird fluttering among the little yellow finch-like weavers may be a lazy whydah using the weavers to hatch its own eggs. Yard workers have to cut the palm branches back to the heart of the tree to make them go away. One of the first questions Doug asked us was whether our boys had packed a BB gun. Unfortunately, "No."

Before I came to Nigeria, an ant was an ant. Varieties here are endless, from the tiny little hair-like ones almost invisible to the big soldiers with fearsome pinchers. The smallest kind have a propensity for sugar and usually go unnoticed till they're surfing our drinks. Tom protects our sugar bowl by keeping it on top the cookstove. If a dessert is not refrigerated immediately, he places it on top of something that can rest in a pan of water forming a moat.

A missionary joke asks, "How can you tell whether a missionary is on his first term, second term, or third term?" The answer: A first termer screams, "There's a bug in my glass!" and pours it out. The second termer quietly lifts out the bug with his spoon, then drinks. The third termer glances at the bug and downs it all. I'm progressing rapidly.

"Line ants" travel in long columns kept carefully in check by soldiers with big pinchers on each side of the line -- and pity the unfortunate soul who gets in their way! They're fond of night travel so we always carry a "torch" (flashlight) and step cautiously.

The first Sunday Bryants were here we were all coming up the hill from evening worship when Rees suddenly burst ahead into our house and ran straight to the bathroom. All was so quiet I was fearful that he had been overcome by "Traveler's Disease" when he cracked the door to yell , "Tell Patti to bring me another pair of pants. I'd forgotten about line ants."

Everyone has a line ant story to tell. One night I had just crawled into bed when I felt a bite -- then another -- and another. I got up and lit a candle. The net above me hung heavy with ants, and the outer wall of the bedroom was covered. I phoned Doug on our intercom, "Sorry to wake you up."

"That's okay. I had to get up and answer the phone anyway."

Then he told me to push back the nets, put on repellent, and set my bedposts in water. "Forget them and go back to sleep," he assured me. "By morning they'll all be gone. Don't spray. It only confuses them and they scatter."

After three nights of the same, I ended their nocturnal journeys through my house by pouring kerosene around it. Where could all these thousands of ants be headed so furiously!

Some white ants (David would say "termites") make hills six feet, or more, high bringing soil up from below the top sandy loam to mix with their saliva so it hardens like concrete. The other day David learned the "hard way." He decided to climb one, lost his grip, and also some skin off his tummy. Fortunately no ants (or "termites") came out of their house to greet him.

We have an abundance of cheap tropical fruit -- pineapple at 10 pence, oranges at two pence a pound, bananas a pence a pound. A vegetable man comes to the door bringing fresh vegetables grown in Northern Nigeria. The cabbage and carrots are sweeter than in America. Potatoes are small, soft, and don't keep well. At present four stalks of bananas hang in our shed -- all dashes.

We buy whole dried milk which the children won't drink without chocolate. I get "agriculture eggs" and sometimes dressed chickens from the state-operated poultry farm. "Bush eggs" from the local free-range chickens have more flavor. Last week I got two Ag-farm rabbits -- one for eating and one for petting. Our carpenter made a hutch and the children are really thrilled to have a pet.

We frequently receive bush chickens for preaching. The pressure cooker should handle any worms or parasites they might have. Last week one church gave Henry a goat kid – great barbecued! Our cook doesn't mind dressing live animals because he takes all the parts we don't want for his own soup pot.

As I write our kids are excitedly watching a Fulani cow (zebu type breed) being pulled and prodded down our road toward the village, probably for a funeral feast. Beef is too expensive for the average daily diet. Cattle are not raised locally because of the tsetse fly which carries sleeping sickness. The Fulani people of the cooler North raise cattle then drive them hundreds of miles south for our local markets -- that's really dried beef on the hoof!

Love,
Dit

September 17, 1964

Dear folks,

This week our drums arrived back in Port Harcourt, transhipped overland from Ghana. Yesterday we checked them through customs -- another $150; but it will probably be another week before they arrive at the house by lorry. The anticipation builds daily, greater than any Christmas, as the kids recall some other treasure of their past and ask if I had packed it.

Meanwhile, I've kept busy sewing linens, shopping for beds and larger desks, and supervising carpenters as they install more shelves, towel racks, etc. to accommodate our family. We have the largest family yet to work here both in size and number.

Time appears to be the most expendable commodity here, but Henry is hopeful for some kind of clinic by the first of the year. Twenty-six villages have signed a pledge to raise 3000 pounds together before January 1. (A Nigerian pound is about $3.) That's an enormous amount for them, but they are counting on the palm fruit harvest. Palm oil extracted from the fruit of the palm oil tree is the chief export of this area.

Henry is taking the articles of incorporation to a lawyer today. Already a large tract of land adjoining the compound for the BTC has been set aside by the villages for medical use.

The fact that backdoor practice is illegal has not stopped the sick from trying. Every morning we awaken to a shed full hoping to be seen. Henry has been doling out a few malaria and pain pills and sending those in need of in-patient care to the nearest hospitals, about eleven miles.

Working at other hospitals gives him a good opportunity to learn about Nigerian medical practice and tropical diseases. One of the most interesting surgeries was finger trimming day at the Itu leprosarium. Twice a week he drives about 50 miles to Queen Elizabeth Hospital, Umuahia. He continues preaching every Sunday and beginning today will teach two classes a week at the BTC.

The children have just about worn out the few books and games we brought with us, but they've been quite happy with so many new things to grab their attention. Also they have seven playmates on campus and the pet rabbit. Marty ties a loop around the rabbit's waist and takes him for a walk or wraps him in a doll blanket and pushes him around in a doll carriage. He takes it all very calmly.

Paul is the only one without another friend his age. He accompanies his dad on all shopping and preaching trips and they are learning chess together.

David spends most of his time on his hands and knees studying the ants. His insect collection grows by the day to the fascination of the other children. He chases crickets to feed his praying mantis pets.

Late summer here is actually cooler than in the States, but the humidity can be oppressive. Wet season continues, and I do mean WET. Henry had not worn his summer suit since our arrival and I found it covered with mold this week.

I really enjoy the fresh vegetables -- cabbage, carrots, green beans, tomatoes, okra, eggplant, and greens. There are others new to me, but Tom is helping me find ways to make them palatable to my family. One, a long squash called marrow, Tom said was a British favorite, so I asked him to cook it the way they enjoyed it. Forget that one! It was as tasteless as other typical British fare. My favorite is the leaf of the fluted pumpkin. Cooked like turnip greens, they're even better.

Communication is a two way street -- so the kids' English books emphasize. I don't know about the Nigerians, but I'm still struggling with my half. Many Nigerians eager to please may act as if they've understood what I've said when really they haven't or are like me, too embarrassed to admit they don't know what was said.

Their speech is peppered with a lot of Pidgin expressions. Whether for emphasis, clarity, or just custom, some words are often doubled. A small thing may be "small-small," or a penny become "penny-penny," etc. Rather than the comparative "very much," I hear "too much." One got carried away and said, "I like it three much." They don't go to get wood or water; they go "for" wood or water. But to "go for bush" means a trip into the bushes for latrine purposes.

Some of the words so strange to us date back to the advent of the Portuguese, the first white people in West Africa, in the fifteenth century. "Dash," a gift or to give, came from the Portuguese verb "das" meaning to give, "sabby" or "savvy" from "sabeir" meaning to know, and "pikin" (pronounced PEEK-in), meaning children, from their word for small. Legend says that the local word referring to white people, pronounced BECK-aye, was the name of the first white person seen in this area. If so, that one probably spelled his name "Beckque."

Ibo (or Igbo) is a tonal language with vowels having the same sounds as in Spanish, i.e. the "i" is pronounced like a long "e," the "e" like a long "a," etc. So words like "his" come out as "hees." When Oxford English flowered with Pidgin and African phonics and intonation comes at me on the fast track, I'm lost.

One British lady commented to Mary Lou Curry, "Oh, they will never learn to speak proper English, just like you Americans," which I concluded was a statement that said more about the speaker than the Nigerians and Americans.

When I can't understand what Tom has said after I've asked him the third time to repeat, I leave the room to ponder. If I still can't figure it out, then I return and approach the subject from a different angle. Once I even found myself speaking to him in Spanish and unaware of it. I guess it seemed right because it's the only foreign language I know -- *pocito,* that is. To my surprise, it was then that I learned Tom had cooked for the Spanish on the off-shore island, Fernando Po. He understood me! No wonder he's such a great cook!

Love,
Dit

Oct. 4, 1964

Dear folks,

Ten days ago our barrels arrived -- all eleven! Two days later the school books came. Since then I have been head over heels (literally heels over head since the top of the barrels are waist high on me) trying to unpack and start school at the same time. After all the stories we'd heard about lost and looted drums, I greeted each as it came off the lorry like a long lost friend. All the locks and spot welding on the lids paid off.

As the crowbar broke open the lids one by one, the kids flitted from one treasure to next. Old toys suddenly became new. The few things I had packed to have something new, I quietly hid for Christmas. The other children on the compound are just as happy for a big assortment of toys and books new to them.

At the time I was packing I agonized over whether it was right to ask the church to pay for shipping some things that had seemed frivolous at the time. Now I am thankful for it all. In fact, if I were to do it again I'd probably put in even more. The kids laughed at how tightly I'd packed every vacant space. When they pulled the top off a toy periscope, out fell all their marbles and little plastic animals.

Many of things I shipped could be found here if I were to wait long enough, shop enough places, and pay twice the price (or more). But I don't have the time, patience, nor money.

Rees came over when we were opening the barrels and said, "Let me just stand here and smell awhile." I thought it was funny until he added, "It smells just like an American five-and-ten. When you've been here awhile, and everything has taken on a musty odor, you'll understand."

The kids have been eager for a large plastic swimming pool I put in for Lee's birthday. Weather-wise now is the perfect time for it, but with the rains ending, it will take a lot of head buckets from the stream to fill it.

Summer months, wet season here, were very humid, but the rains and cloud cover helped shield us from the direct tropical sun. Now dry season is upon us! "Dry" simply means that the rains have stopped. The humidity is still with us, and our sun shield is gone. Without electric fans days are oppressive, but nights usually cool enough to sleep well.

October! Oh, to see the glorious scarlet and golden hills of Southern Indiana! I miss them so much it hurts! I try instead to concentrate on the immediate.

As a whole our area is mostly monotonous fairly flat land. Our house happens to be on one hillside of a stream, and it has been interesting to sit on our front porch and watch the rain advancing from the opposite hill. The trees are mostly palms interspersed with a few locust and "cotton" (kapok) trees. The huge tropical forests of the past have been destroyed to plant cassava and yam. The soil is sandy loam so that it washes badly during the torrents of rain. In fact Doug asked me, "Have you noticed that there are no rocks?" He had tried in vain to find a pebble to skip across the stream. Henry likes to say, "It has a beauty all its own." But there's nothing here that says, "Home," to me.

It's Sunday afternoon and all the children are down at the school building where Patti Bryant and Charla Lawyer are having Bible class for about 100 village children. Ours, even the older ones, enjoy the old stories with a new approach and learning familiar songs in Ibo.

Now, I can see everyone pouring out of the building gleefully waving their papers. That means it's time for my Bible class with our school age children. I'll finish later.

Late p.m. Henry found enough ice in Aba this afternoon to make two freezers of ice cream -- thanks to the crank freezer I had packed. We invited all the families on campus to celebrate the arrival of our drums with us. Now only Sara, who is spending the night with Marty, remains.

October 1 was Republic Day, the national holiday celebrating independence from Britain in 1960. The Bryants and the Farrars took off for the Atlantic beach. After driving for about three hours over very rough roads (rough even by Nigerian standards), we reached the mouth of the Qua Ibo River. There we had to bargain with the owners of a dugout for the 30 min. ride on to the ocean. It seemed like some kind of African fantasy as we glided downstream -- the stillness broken only by the boatmen singing in Efik to the rhythm of their paddles and unrecognizable bird sounds echoing from the bordering mangrove swamps. The river was so wide that the opposite bank was only a faint green line on the horizon.

When we reached the beach, we told the men when to return but did not pay them until we were safely back to where we'd left the car. We'd taken enough food for a picnic dinner and supper and returned home late. The next day the kids spent hours washing, counting, and arranging their shell collections -- and begging to go back soon.

Calvert school material seems excellent, but very time consuming. The schedule for each grade is outlined as if that one were my only student. Every afternoon I spend about two hours going over the lessons and coordinating schedules for the next day in order to have individual time with the one who may need help while the others do assignments alone. Hopefully, I'll become more efficient. Right now, as a first-time teacher, I'm the one learning the most. I feel satisfied that they are getting a better education, and definitely more attention, than they would be receiving in America -- if the teacher survives!

I'm applying for a Nigerian driver's license by virtue of my American one, though I will probably never get up enough nerve to face this traffic situation. Not only would I have to master a standard shift and learn to drive on the "wrong" side of the road, but also how to dodge all the lorries, taxis, cyclists, and pedestrians on narrow, congested roads. The horn is the most useful part of the car. Meeting another vehicle usually means moving onto a narrow shoulder ("verge") full of ruts and people.

The Nigerian love for religious mottos is displayed in huge letters on every lorry or "mammy-wagon" (so-called because of all the women with their produce riding to and from market). A vehicle is identified by its motto, e.g. the "Why Worry" bus. The irony of it strikes you when you've just been pushed off the road by the "I Leave Everything to God" lorry.

Speaking of names, Nigerians also like Bible names and words for their children e.g. Mark, Mary, Joseph, Love, Joy, Blessing. Some names would seem sacrilegious to us like Emanuel and Chuku or Chi (Ibo names for God). Sometimes names are descriptive of the days or conditions of birth like Okpara (first born) or Icon (born in the night), and there seems to be no end to the Mondays, Fridays, and Sundays. I've yet to meet the other weekdays.

To distinguish so many with the same name we often use their work as their last name -- John Carpenter, John Washerman, Friday Cook, etc. -- the way our own surnames began. A Nigerian wife annexes her husband's first name. I learned that when I kept receiving letters addressed to "Mrs. Grace Henry."

The parents usually give their child one name, the second being his father's name and the third his grandfather's, etc. Our steward, Monday John Akpakpan, explained to me that his name was Monday, his father's was John, and his grandfather's was Akpakpan. Thus his brother Timothy goes by the name Timothy John Akpakpan. When I asked Monday how far back he could go with the names of ancestors, he threw his head back and laughed, "All the way to Noah, Madam."

The children are all well and happy. They enjoy helping David find new bugs. Paul is usually so lost in a book we plan to give him a bicycle for his birthday hoping it will encourage him to get out more. Lee says to tell Grandpa, "Yes. Yes." He misses all that teasing.

Love,
Dit

October 18, 1964

Dear folks,

Because Henry preached at a nearby village today, the whole family went with him for the first time. Nigerians appreciate children and were happy to see us as a family. I was afraid we'd be a distraction, but they appeared to hang onto every word.

I wish there was a way I could describe their singing. Some Ibo songs resemble chants, but all have distinctive African rhythms and runs. Doug said that when Andy T. Ritchie, Jr. from Harding was here he kept saying, "Oh, that syncopation!" Worshipping with them was a great spiritual experience. (I told Henry later that if we could just can some of those church songs, he could finance a hospital by selling them to the American teenagers.)

If I've organized well the day before, we finish school by noon. Afternoons are too hot to concentrate anyway. Even local schools dismiss then. Lee prefers learning the alphabet and numbers along with Hank in the first grade to his own kindergarten. The workers know to tell anyone asking to see me that I am unavailable until noon except for emergencies, or else I'd never get through. We make school serious business.

By the way, school readiness for Nigerian children, who have no birth certificates, is determined by whether they can reach across their heads and touch the opposite ear. Sounds ridiculous, I know, but it really is a good gage of physical development not usually reached till about age 6.

Last week we went to Enugu, our capital in the Eastern Region, to see the Ministry of Health officials about our hospital plans and to inquire about well drilling. We also enjoyed visiting the Curry and Keesee families who've worked there since August. We learned that it will cost approximately $4500 to get a well dug and about the same to hook on to NEPA (Nigerian Electrical Power Authority). An American has already ordered a Sears water pump for us.

The local people continue bringing a few Nigerian pounds as they are able, and we keep it for them in our safe. So far they have given about $300. Without banks in the villages the people really have no safe place to keep money away from thieves. If they don't spend it, they risk losing it. Some form cooperatives into which each gives equally each month as a way of saving for a larger expense. Each month the lump sum will be distributed to one of the contributors, rotating through the membership. Usually when they need money between pay periods, they ask for an advance. I keep a record of what I have paid out during the month. Sometimes there is nothing left for payday.

Last week we had a surprise visit from a North Carolina family sent here by Indian Head Mills to open a textile mill in Aba. They say there will be about 25 American families coming to Aba. They accepted the job because of the pay incentive, but the company had done so little to prepare them that they were astonished to learn that all Nigerian citizens are black.

Because I wanted Halloween to be a tradition of fun for the family, we put up the few decorations I had brought in our living room one evening, plus a few homemade ones. The next morning Monday walked in, glanced around at all the bats, skull, etc., and said, "This place looks like a ju-ju house." The idea had never occurred to me. Monday is knowledgeable about us crazy Americans and our holidays, but when a Nigerian official came to the house to see Henry, I quickly swooped them all down before his visit. The kids have great ideas for making costumes when they "trick-or-treat" the other two families.

Patti Bryant's father, Dr. F.W. Mattox, president of Lubbock Christian College, will be coming soon. In preparation, Rees has rented the Aba town hall and has been advertising a lectureship by an American university president. Hopefully this will put us in contact with the educated people of Aba. One night during his visit will be set aside for a missionary retreat.

Phil Dunn, his wife, and three preschool children arrived this month from Indiana to work at the Ukpom Bible College -- another Hoosier!

I'm sure the kids' American friends must wonder what ours find to do in a place where there is "no place to go" and no TV. Before I left America I made plans for Paul and David to get Lone Scout cards so they can continue with badges. I have organized a Girl Scout Troop on Foreign Soil (TOFS) for Marty, Shauna Lawyer, and Sara Bryant. We applied to be TOFS # 1 in Nigeria, but learned that a troop in Lagos beat us to it. So we are # 2. I brought all the necessary books and materials, even blank badges so they could embroider their own troop crest. We've chosen a palm with French knot coconuts. For David I made a bug net using mosquito netting and found dry cleaning fluid in the market for his bug killing jars. Hank and Lee are interested in everything.

We went Christmas shopping at the Ikot Ekpene raffia market (said to be the world's largest raffia market), about 10 miles inside Ibibio land, for ebony carvings, raffia products and other native crafts to send home. Mailing a box from here is very involved. Just finding a sturdy box is hard enough. Besides all the forms listing contents and value, they have packaging regulations about how to wrap and tie, covering every knot with old-fashioned red sealing wax. We get it in Aba market, heat it with a candle, and drip it onto the knots -- British system, I presume. Since letters can take a month, who knows how long for a package, or in what condition it might arrive -- if at all. Just wanted you to know that we thought of you.

Love,
Dit

November 1, 1964

Dear folks,

The weeks fly! Monday through Friday it's school in the mornings, checking papers and organizing for the next day in the afternoons, and all the while supervising the household workers. Saturdays are for shopping and trying to catch up on what I've neglected. Sundays are always crammed -- church, Bible classes, and usually company. We enjoy Americans from Port Harcourt and Aba who come for church and fellowship.

As I write it's 4 p.m. Sunday. About one hundred village children who came to the school building for Bible classes are lingering along the roadside to watch ours on the swings and monkey bars in our front lawn. I can imagine how much they'd love to try them, but how could you possible supervise what so many might decide to do. Paul is out on his new birthday bike. It's adult size, Nigerian style with a bell and hand brakes -- a real car here. And is he ever proud of it!

Yesterday everyone went to the Port Harcourt Airport, about 50 miles, to meet Dr. F. W. Mattox at the airport. We left early to take the kids to Christmas Toyland at Kingsway, a new two-story department store -- really "uptown" compared with Aba market. They have fun just riding the escalator (the only one in this region). Patti had told me that I should consider buying anything I thought the kids would like for Christmas because it probably wouldn't be around later. Pickings looked meager to me, but she couldn't believe the selections available now compared to those of her previous tours.

In the afternoon Henry and the other men went golfing with Floyd Young, a Christian who is supervising the construction of the Port Harcourt petroleum refinery, while his wife Marie took the rest of us to the pool. One of the plums offered to their expatriate employees by foreign companies is membership in private clubs. Later we met for a picnic before going to the airport. A real mini-vacation!

This afternoon Henry and Doug are in Aba distributing announcements for the upcoming lectureship featuring Dr. Mattox. A large delegation of Christians have gathered at the school to sing him their welcome. Tomorrow following Dr. Mattox's lecture for the Ukpom Bible students, all the missionary families in this area will join in a pot luck meal.

The Aba lecture is scheduled for Tuesday evening and Wednesday will be the day for our retreat. Dr. Mattox will be leaving

Saturday a.m. To make the most of his visit we've made the whole week a school holiday. Finally a school schedule that can be tailored to the family schedule!

The kids have had a Halloween unlike any other. Our Girl Scouts baked and decorated cookies. Since Dr. Mattox would be arriving on the 31st, we made the 30th our trick-or-treat night. The workers thought their home-made costumes were hilarious and gave the kids oranges when they appeared at their quarters. But the three missionary interns went all out. They gave the kids Hacks cough drops which look like candy, but taste awful. Then as the kids were going across the campus, the interns covered in sheets flapping in the wind came tearing behind them with terrifying screams. One snatched up Paul and ran in circles with Paul over his shoulder looking more like a body than a person. The kids screamed their head off. One even had to take time out for a change of clothes. Later when they met at our house for cookies and drinks, they declared in one voice, "It was the most fun Halloween we ever had!"

Monday p.m. -- The children and I stayed home from Ukpom because we have drippy noses ("catarrh" here). It's just as well. The place has been a beehive of activity all day. Lorries have been delivering sand, gravel, and cement for the nurses' house (Henry's having one of the servants' quarters remodeled for them). A bamboo shed with a palm thatch roof was constructed to protect the bags of cement in case of rain. I stopped to count how many people were working inside our house -- seven! That included painters, carpenters, and a glazier (replacing window panes broken before our arrival). That's privacy, Nigerian style!

I couldn't count the cups of tea I've served recently to visiting dignitaries coming to welcome Henry and offer their assistance with his plans for a hospital -- the Minister of Internal Affairs, the local chiefs, the headmaster of a local school, and delegations bringing funds. Henry has requested permission to convert an old government rest house built for travelling district officers in the British colonial days into a temporary dispensary. The building had also been home for Bill and Gerry Nicks and their girls when they first came to Iboland to begin the Bible school while their own house was being built. It's frustrating for Henry to see such desperate medical needs and be so helpless to do anything about them when he has the ability.

The children are enjoying school more than they had in America. And I can't believe how much I have learned! What more enjoyable way to spend my time! In America I did housework all day while someone else had my children. Here I have them all day while someone else is doing the housework. I get to know them in a way never before possible.

Egrets, a sure sign of the approaching dry season, have appeared on campus. They follow the cattle in the cooler, arid North to feast on cattle ticks and the insects stirred up by the cattle. In dry season they migrate south and enjoy our frogs, insects, and lizards. I haven't yet figured out why because insects and frogs seem more plentiful in wet season. Whatever prompts them doesn't matter. They are so graceful and quiet, I'm happy to exchange them for the noisy weavers of wet season.

I've been collecting information on gardening in Nigeria. The tropical flowers are gorgeous. I've just planted a double red hibiscus and plan to try many more.

The kids are writing letters to enclose with mine.

Love,
Dit

Children's Letters to their Grandparents

Looking through their Grandmother's letters, I was delighted to find the children's letters --so typical of their personalities. Here they are just as they were written.

From Paul, turning 12, fascinated with facts:

November 2, 1964

Dear Grandma,

I am happy here in Africa.

The Bryants have a new carport. They also have their barrels.

Saturday we went to Port harcourt to meet Mr. Mattox. He is the president of Lubbock Christian College. He is also the Bryants' grandfather.

There are big piles of sand and gravel for the nurses' home. We also have forty bags of cement in our garage.

Love,
Paul

(A diagram of the campus was enclosed)

From Marty, 10, creative, eager to learn:

> Dearest Grandma,
> How are you and Grandpa getting along? We have the sore throat going around are family.
> I'm in the fifth grade now and am getting along fine with my Calvert School Course. I have three interesting books to read. They are called Robin Hood, King Arthur, and Arabian Nights, also a poetry book called The Singing World.
> Yours truly,
Marty F.
>
> P.S. Remember me to everyone.

From David, almost 9, the family biologist, in bug heaven:

> Dear Grandmother and Grandfather ther shur is a lot of insects. Ther are click bettles two inches loung.Ther are lots of dragenflys whos three inches wingspred. I have not seen any stag bettles or staghorn bettles. I have seen one bee. Over hear you may see a butteful butterfly every day. I have a moth that is 5 1/2 inches in wingspread. Ther is an ant with pinchers longer than its head that is 1/8 of an inch loung. The pinchers are like this (diagram enclosed). Another kind of ant has pinchers two 1/8 inch loung like this (another diagram). Another kind of ant has a head like this (diagram).Ther are praying mantases that I make pets of. Ther are buteful grasshoppers with red eyes yellow legs and blue wings.
> love
David

Finally, probably Hank's first letter, written in manuscript except his name in blocks:

> Ndewo.*
> I'm in first grade. I'm learning to read.
> love HANK
>
> *An Ibo greeting

The following letter written by Henry to the mission committee of the West End Church of Christ is included because it explains a significant change in our decision as to the best way to begin a medical clinic.

It was written after our conferences with Dr. Mattox and with the consensus of our coworkers.

HENRY FARRAR, M.D. F.A.C.S.
Box 823
Aba, Nigeria, Africa

November 7, 1964

Mission committee
Church of Christ
3334 West End Ave.
Nashville, Tennessee 37205, USA
Dear Brethren:

It continues to be a pleasure to work for the Lord in Nigeria. Every day we are impressed with the "open door" in the hearts and minds of the Nigerians to the gospel of Jesus Christ. Whether we speak in the market place or to the educated leaders at the Town Hall, we have been getting a good hearing. For example, we had over 100 leaders of the people to hear Dr. F. W. Mattox on Tuesday night. He is president of Lubbock Christian College and is visiting here as he journeys to Japan and Okinawa to preach for the Armed Forces there. We had a few invitation cards printed and mailed out to the leaders, and with that scanty preparation with only a few days notice, a hundred came. They came and they listened raptly and they asked intelligent questions. Yesterday I went with Brother Mattox and we preached to over 200 in the market place. After a couple of hours we had to leave and return home with those people still asking questions and grasping for literature. Brethren we cannot neglect the tremendous "open door" in Nigeria. God will bless all who hear the cry of these people for truth.

A little progress is being made in my four-fold work. First I help Grace rear our five children. Yesterday Brother Mattox baptized into Christ our daughter Marty. We had a beautiful service at the little stream of water at the bottom of the hill here. We feel our children have some advantage as they see this work and help a little. Paul who is now twelve goes with me on appointments. Second I have the privilege of teaching four hours a week in the Bible Training College. The men we teach are undoubtedly the hope of Nigeria as we try to help them develop into gospel preachers. Third I preach at two or three congregations each Sunday morning. We arrange appointments three months in advance. The people respect what the white men say and they receive us with considerable enthusiasm. Fourth I am able to take care of some sick people. I perform surgery two days a week from dawn till dusk at Queen Elizabeth Hospital, Umuahia, 36 miles away. We are getting arrangements made now to begin out-patient work at a nearby building owned by the government and loaned to us for that purpose.

To tell the truth we are a little frustrated from the medical work point of view. The people need care so badly. They come to the back door of our house and beg for help. It is unwise to do "back porch medicine." Yet the local government which should build the hospital is moving ever so slowly. Many of the leaders are often apathetic to the needs of their people. The poor who need the hospital, many of whom are brethren in Christ, are trying with all their power to get the hospital. A preacher brought 6 shilling of his own money the other day (84 cents). We get similar contributions every day or so. So far about $1200 has been brought and there is considerable doubt that the promised minimum amount to begin construction will be brought. We doubt if we should begin with less than $3000.

After considerable discussion and thought, we now have the opinion that we should raise our own money, build our own hospital and control it completely. Since this is somewhat different from the original plan to have the Nigerians build the hospital, I will outline some of the considerations which have led us to this option.

In the first place the more money contributed to the building by the Nigerians, the more control and possible interference we will encounter in the work. Some denominational mission doctors here have decried how ill-informed local officials who have a voice in the hospital control have sometimes interfered with the proper operation of the hospital. If we build our own, we can be freed from a lot of frustrating negotiations. With complete control by Christians, administration will be easier. In making alliance with the local government, there might be some yoking together with unbelievers.

The most powerful chiefs are practically always polygamists. By saying this, we are not discouraged with these people. ...

Second, for only $45,000 we can build a creditable hospital. If we could get ten or fifteen Christians to give up the price of a new car, we could have a hospital here and now controlled entirely by Christians... The walls would be concrete block and the floor concrete -- their houses mostly have mud floors. Having investigated many hospitals here, we are very confident that we can build a satisfactory 30 bed hospital for $45,000 including water, electricity, operating room, maternity, clinic, pharmacy, laboratory and two fifteen bed wards.

Third, we are convinced that right here at the Bible Training College is the ideal location for the hospital. First, we will be in an area central for the people of 600 churches of Christ. Second, we will be in a location for our missionary families from America enabling them to be somewhat free from health worries with a doctor nearby. Third, we are settled down in a nice house here in the American missionary community. If we move to another location, we will have to add the cost of building a house for us to the bill. While other communities might be able to build a hospital, such communities are generally inaccessible and off the beaten track. Fourth, Brother Lawyer and Brother Bryant here at the Bible Training College have had considerable experience in building and they would be able to supervise the construction here.

I will admit that it has been very hard on my conscience to see very sick people at the back door begging for medical help I can give, and then I have to tell them to go because we have no facilities to treat the sick here. It is hard to get across the point to a mother with a dying child. The $1200 they have brought is a tremendous sacrifice for them. We are not interested in a "big give away program". We just want to help these people who are trying to help. We charge fees to cover expenses and costs so it will not be a "give away program."

Brethren, will you please respond to these questions? Because of the time already passed, the possibility of corrupt men hindering our work if we depend on Nigerian officials, the long delays we see ahead because of this, and the great urgency both in meeting the needs of these people and in receiving the benefits this service will bring in influencing whole new segments of this society for Christ, I feel I must ask you for specific guidance.

1. Do you agree that we should build our own facilities and control the policies? (Local and federal help in some quantity can still be had, even if we make the original $45,000 investment.)

2. If you agree that we should build and control our own hospital (and all of us here now agree that this is the wise procedure), how should the $45,000 be raised? We see several possibilities:

    a. The money is not needed all at one time. What we need is a definite plan and assurance. With a promise we could begin now to make concrete blocks with what we have and money could be sent over the construction time of several months. This would save precious time and lives.

    b. West End church might accept this additional project and give all the $45,00 or give part and raise the balance.

    c. Those of us here could accept this challenge, ask West End church for a single commitment, then print a brochure and start mailing fund raising letters. This would be a long process and indefinite. It would take a great deal of time needed here. The missionaries here would prefer that you relieve us of this burden, but are ready to take it on if it is your judgment we should do so.

Brethren, will you please give this your prayerful consideration and give us definite and clear guidance as to the course you want us to pursue.

                      Faithfully yours,
                        Henry Farrar, M.D., F.A.C.S.

Copies to Bro. McInteer and Dr. Cayce

November 8, 1964

Dear folks,

Paul began his letter to a friend in Johnson City with a paragraph of one sentence, "I am happy here." I guess that about sums up the situation for us all, though I really do miss autumn.

Just when I thought it wasn't possible, the daytime weather has become even more uncomfortable. Life in Nigeria does have its compensations though. There was never a more friendly, appreciative people than the Nigerians or more congenial neighbors than the

Lawyers and the Bryants. And I enjoy the freedom of not being tied to a clock or pocket calendar!

Marty has been talking about wanting to be baptized for several weeks, but I really didn't encourage her for fear she might not understand at age 10. While Dr. Mattox was here we suggested she have a private discussion with him, and he told us, "If she were my daughter, I would not hesitate a minute to baptize her." So Friday we all went downhill to the stream where he baptized her. Marty has always been such a sweet, unselfish, tender-hearted child. It is no surprise she wants to give her life to Jesus at such a young age. I entered November 6 in my date book as her spiritual birthday.

We meet every evening with Dr. Mattox for his advice about our problems on the field and his suggestions for the future. The chief topic on the agenda has been how to get the hospital underway. The government won't help until we can come up with a five or ten year plan, and we are still waiting on financial support locally. Now at the end of three months, the villages have raised approximately $400 of the $8000 promised by January 1. One poor preacher, in debt himself, made a special trip to bring a donation of six shillings (about 84 cents).

The lecture at the Aba town hall was entitled "The True Meaning of Education." This was our first effort to reach out to the business and professional community, and the response was tremendous. Their attentiveness and the quality of questions asked during the question session were very impressive.

Brother Mattox taught every day in the Bible school and was impressed with the students' thirst for knowledge and their spiritual maturity. He said he had thought he knew a lot about the work here through Rees and Patti, but what he had seen completely changed his whole outlook for the better.

At our school lectureship one of the speakers was Moses Opara, the converted ju-ju priest who is now a missionary himself in the Muslim north where his life is in danger. His lesson, "Go and Tell" would have put many American preachers to shame. I had heard about Moses before coming to Nigeria, but this week I met him for the first time. His piercing eyes, his glowing countenance, and his confident bearing would impress anyone.

While Dr. Mattox was here, the Bryants' septic tank stopped up. Dr. Mattox, so capable that he had built his own house in Searcy, dug up the problem himself. Rees said the most valuable lesson Dr. Mattox taught the Bible students during his time here was when they saw a university president getting dirty unstopping a septic tank. The prevailing goal for education seems to be freedom from manual labor and the most humble service.

We appreciate having someone of his experience and practical wisdom here to look at our efforts objectively. We still laugh at his answer when asked what he thought about our having college students as missionary internes, "It will do them a world of good, and I don't believe it will hurt the Nigerians very much." As a result of all our discussions with him, Henry is sending a reassessment of our plans to the mission committee at West End.

As manager of our "utility company," Doug place the generator house near the stream as far away from the house as possible to lessen the noise. In the tropics daylight and dark are almost equally twelve hours year round -- 6 a.m. to 6 p.m. daylight without dawn or dusk as we know it. Doug has taught our "watch nights" to turn on the generator when they arrive at 6 p.m. Rotating weekly families turn it off at 10 p.m. with switches he had installed in each house. If we need lights after 10, we can notify the family in charge that we will turn off the generator, or we can use candles or a pressurized kerosene Tilley lamp kept trimmed and filled by our steward.

While our running cold water runs up the hill on the heads of water carriers, our running hot water runs in a large teakettle from the kitchen stove to the bathroom with the one who wants a bath. One person described her bathing process as soaping with the water in front of her, then turning around to rinse with the water in back.

Wednesday the Currys, who had come from Enugu for the retreat, helped us celebrate Paul's twelfth birthday in the evening, then spent the night. When we had the kids settled for the night, Mary Lou put her kettle on to heat. She and I became so engrossed in our tete-a-tete we forgot about time. Suddenly it hit us! 10 o'clock, and we'd not phoned for a delay! She dashed to the kitchen for her kettle. Just as she started her race down the hall to the bathroom, hot kettle in hand, all suddenly went pitch black. Her spontaneous scream reverberated across the campus through the night stillness. The ensuing hush was broken by the phone when a very concerned Doug cautiously asked, "Is everything all right over there?"

We lit candles and ended our day with a good laugh.

Love,
Dit

November 19, 1964

Dear folks,

As the rains decrease, the temperature increases! Our egret flock now numbers twenty. They're such fun to watch, especially when one catches a toad. The greedy flock descends on him, and a tug of war ensues.

Kids will be kids. It's astounding how "isolation" develops creativity! Right now I'm at Henry's desk watching the Farrar, Bryant, and Lawyer kids on the screened play porch in front of me at their favorite pretend game, "Animal Land." Using legos, blocks, plastic animals and whatever else is available to build battlegrounds, forts, and castles, they enlist armies and engage in a mix of medieval and modern warfare.

Our home school includes everything our children would be studying in America and more. As teachers we set aside one night a week to listen to them read aloud, recite poetry, or give an oral presentation for our constructive criticism.

Marty, Shauna Lawyer, and Sara Jo Bryant work as hard on Girl Scout projects as if they were a troop of thirty instead of three. Last night the families enjoyed a puppet show written and produced entirely by the girls with help from Paul as the props man. For their service projects they work on Bible school materials for the Nigerian children's classes and are making Christmas toys for a Nigerian teacher's family of eight. They are also planning a hobby show with all the enthusiasm of exhibiting at a county fair although only their own families will get to enjoy it.

Doug Lawyer had a tennis court, a barbecue pit, and a concrete picnic table (wood quickly succumbs to termites) made on campus. A boy of Paul's age from the Aba textile group will be spending the weekend. To celebrate his and David's birthdays, we're having a wiener roast -- a rare treat. Hot dogs are expensive and scarce, but we found some in Port Harcourt.

Our MK's (missionary kids) are really privileged, not deprived. Could there be a better way to develop a concept of world evangelism and an appreciation for other cultures? Joyce Huffard Harrison, the first second-generation missionary to return to Nigeria, arrived recently with her husband Don to work at Ukpom -- a missionary parent's dream, to see the work continue through their children.

Our extra furniture has been slowly taking shape. John Igwe, the carpenter, estimates costs from our diagrams and bargains for the raw wood at the Aba lumber market. Pop would really get a kick out of watching the Aba "sawmills" -- unlike anything he ever operated. Four or five crosscut saws are started through a log from one end. Little by little the men move first one and then the other, proceeding down the full length of the log to turn out rough boards. After bargaining for the lumber, John has to negotiate with a lorry driver to bring the lumber to our compound. Without power tools, he planes, saws, and nails until we have the finished piece. That's why carpenters become full time employees. But lumber is never really seasoned in this high humidity, and the finished product changes with the seasons.

West Africa does produce some beautiful woods -- mahogany, ebony, rosewood, and others -- but none of these grow in our immediate area. The biggest trees amid our palms -- kapok and iroko -- are often spared for the spirits believed to be residing in them. On special days animists sacrifice to those trees. John boasts that he knows wood, and iroko is his favorite for furniture -- a wood so hard I bend nails trying to hang anything.

A painter also works almost full time on campus. Our house was due a fresh paint job inside and out. As I watched the painter go over the walls with a three-inch brush, I wished I had packed a roller in our drums. Thinking one might have made it to Aba market, I tried to describe a paint roller. He just shook his head incredulously.

I was so tired one night I stopped to wonder why. That day I'd had one painter working inside the house and another on the outside, a mason repairing cracks in the wall due to settling, a cook in the kitchen, a steward cleaning the house, a washerman doing the laundry, one yardman cutting grass and the other carrying water, a carpenter putting up rods for new curtains, and a tailor doing the mending I'd not had time to do.

Although each considers himself a specialist in his field, we don't always have the same ideas about the job. Except for the cook, steward, and yardmen, I find myself constantly running back and forth to check and explain. At the same time I am also teaching four kids in four separate rooms.

As a do-it-myself person, I find it hard to delegate. But since that's a necessary way of life here, I've picked up a few pointers. First, you'd better get it right the first time! It's far easier to think a job through then carefully explain step by step than to reteach, and woe to me if someone has already taught a different way. Why are people so resistant to change! Pride? Inertia? Or maybe the British influence?

Since living here I've discovered the essential difference between British systems and American know-how. The Englishman will say, "We've done it this way for twenty-five years and it works. Why change?" The American will say, "We've done it this way for twenty-five years. There must be a better way!"

Secondly, never assume that they have understood your explanation (or plan to do it your way if they have) no matter how carefully you explain. Appearing to understand can be a way to save face. After carefully explaining to the painter that we wanted a wall to be light blue, I walked into the room later to find half the wall in a vivid chartreuse. He couldn't seem to understand why I demanded he cover it immediately with pale blue. After all, he thought it was beautiful. And he already had the chartreuse paint on hand. Why would I want to spend good money to buy more paint? Give me the mechanical and electrical servants any day! At least they're usually predictable.

To convert the former servants' quarters behind the Bryants' house into a home for the American nurses who plan to come as soon as they get visas, Henry designed the renovations, hired the workers, and used his working funds. Construction costs are less here. Blocks for the house, molded by hand using our own sandy soil and sun dried, are now being laid.

Henry bought a drawing board and drafting tools and works long hours in the evenings on hospital plans. Before government officials will release the old district officer's rest house (which no one has used since the Nicks were there ten years ago) for a temporary dispensary, he is required to present a 10-year plan for a hospital. Their prepared blueprints are expensive and out-dated. His vo-tech art training has equipped him to do a professional drafting job.

So a typical workday in the life of Henry Farrar right now might include any of the following: teaching at the Bible College, performing surgery at Queen Elizabeth or another hospital, treating sick students, meeting with officials, preaching in a market place, overseeing work on a nurses' home, drafting plans for a hospital, writing letters, studying for his Sunday sermons, meeting with the many backdoor visitors, and odd jobs too numerous to mention. We both stay busy!

Love,
Dit

Henry's letter to his family is included for another perspective.

November 22, 1964

Dear Evelyn, George, Carol, and Betty,

You folks have been so good to write us the news. One of the cardinal sins at Onicha Ngwa is to go into Aba and not check the mailbox. With three families here the boxes get checked at least once and sometimes three times a day.

It is hot and humid here, but we are standing it well and nobody has lost any weight. In fact I have gained two pounds. We have not had rain for a week and that's the driest it has been. Even so anything left untouched for a week is covered with mold.

We have considerable difficulty with receiving packages here. The only packages to get through without excessive customs charges are books and magazines. They even charge customs for the postage stamps on the packages. Regular mail takes 6 to 8 weeks, but if things go by air the postage is more so the customs charges are more.

We have beautiful hibiscus and a low broad tree full of pink blossoms in front. The egrets are stalking over the campus getting fat on the bug life here. These birds, about the size of ducks, are perfectly white except for long yellow bills. I guess the wing spread to be about 24 to 36 inches. When they fly they stick their feet straight back and apparently use their small tails as rudders. They twist and turn their long necks in many ways and there are plenty of bugs for them to eat. Our windows attract a fabulous array every night. David is so busy collecting them, he will have a nice collection if mold doesn't destroy his specimens.

We are having a little trouble getting the hospital underway chiefly due to some of the leaders. The poor people are almost without exception friendly and grateful. We have some strong, dependable preachers and the church has advanced tremendously in the ten years of work in Ibo land. The majority of preachers have had no more than five years experience and came out of paganism. If you can imagine America without any preacher who has had more than 8 or 10 years experience, you can see the problem.

This morning was typical of our Sunday mornings. Paul, Roger Rhodes (one of the ministerial interns from Fort Worth), and I visited five congregation near Umuahia. The first two were way out in the bush off the dirt roads, about fifty people meeting in mud buildings. The third had a concrete block building, aluminum roof, and dirt floor. There were about forty members, but no preacher. The fourth church had rented a Union Hall in Umuahia and had a very fine preacher with about four years experience. His pay is about $16/month. The fifth was just out of town, a mud building painted nicely. They also had a good preacher with about two or three years experience. The last two places dashed us eggs, bananas, papayas, and oranges.

Grace works hard teaching the children and it is really a job, I know. We have had the house painted, and the painters and other people coming to the house keep things in an uproar. Actually there is a stream of people from dawn till dusk seeking one thing or another at our door.

Well, this will give you an idea of how things are getting along. Actually things are going fairly smoothly though, of course, a few obstructions along.

Love,
Henry

December 6, 1964

Dear folks,

What a week! The first four days we were in Enugu on business and pleasure. We had been informed that Iris Hays, one of the nurses planning to come, had been denied a visa because our quota was full. For some time we have been trying to get our missionary quota increased from 11 to 33. Request forms required Henry to list the exact positions we needed. The government is willing to accept all but the nurses. (Nurses here are called "Sisters," British term.) They insist there are enough Nigerian sisters and ours might replace Nigerians who need jobs. They fail to recognize that first, there really is a nurse shortage in the existing hospitals and secondly, we are asking for "sister tutor" positions to train more Nigerians nurses rather than replace any. Now we wait for the outcome of our efforts.

Enugu is a very interesting city, a mix of the very affluent and the very poor. We visited Nsukka University with beautiful, modern buildings. We ate our anniversary dinner in the new Presidential Hotel, which outclasses any American hotel where we have dined. In contrast to the bland British fare of most Nigerian restaurants, the cuisine was genuinely French -- even the menu written in French. The price was no more than a good American meal. In that same neighborhood were the homes of the ministers, the governor's palace, and the Assembly Building, all modern and luxurious.

Later we visited the Enugu General Hospital affiliated with the University School of Medicine and were appalled at the poverty and need for medical care. It made us wonder where the U.S. AID funds were really going.

We had a great visit with the Currys. Mary Lou and I would never run out of talk. Henry indulged in civilization's ultimate -- submerging in a hot bath. At the Enugu Market Garden, a government research agricultural station, I found information on gardening in Nigeria and some unusual house plants. Our family toured the pottery where the kids tried their hands and bought souvenirs. I chose a lovely tea set. I've never had, or needed, a tea set before, but it will be very useful here when officials call.

After our return from Enugu, we all went to Port Harcourt to see Joe Cross and his family off, ending their second tour here. Though they have no plans to return, none of us would be surprised to see them back. While filming their departure, I turned around to catch the interpreter who had worked closely with him at Ukpom looking very sad and despondent, shaking his head from side to side. I felt sure the man was saying to himself, "I'll never see them again." How hard it must be for the people who work closely with us to be always saying good-by.

In the Port Harcourt market I found the perfect blue print for my living room couch covers and drapes. I can hardly wait to declare an official school vacation and get to work on them.

We had a kind of family tragedy, certainly one for the kids. One morning we awoke to find the rabbit stiff, stone-cold dead. He had seemed perfectly healthy when Marty had him out to bounce and graze on the grass the afternoon before, so I presume he died of kerosene poisoning. The painters have been cleaning their brushes with kerosene then pouring it on the grass. I don't know why it hadn't occurred to me what might happen, but it didn't. I'm so sorry for Marty, but I don't think we'll try again. If pets get sick here, vet service is lacking, and we do see rabies.

All the missionary families plan to meet on our campus for a Christmas potluck. The adults and children have drawn names separately for a gift exchange. As a farewell gift the Crosses left money for a Christmas turkey (available at Port Harcourt for approx. $1.30/lb). The yardmen are building a palm arbor. It's so exciting for the kids, but believe me, I'd rather see a white Christmas than a green one any day!

Please don't bother to send anything our way, but your prayers and best wishes. The postage on a package would be too much for you and the customs here would be too much for us. The postal workers give us a rough time about packages, demanding invoices for things sent as gifts before they will release them -- even though the value is clearly stated on the outside of the package as required. It's the kind of rudeness that has given rise to a common expression, "post office manners."

When Patti went to claim a Christmas package sent to her children by the grandparents, with no invoice of course, the postal worker opened the box, and emptying it to see how much customs he could charge, he said, "Let's see what's in here."

Pulling out a labeled wrapped gift, he examined it curiously, then asked, "Billy Rees? What's a 'Billy Rees'?"

By then she'd had it! Patti burst into tears crying, "That's my little boy, and that's his Christmas present from his grandparents." It was too much for the man! He threw it all back into the box and shoved it at her, "Take it!" And she came home jubilant!

Love,
Dit

December 29, 1964

Dear folks,

I hope yours was a white Christmas. I'd like to think that somebody got to enjoy one. Ours was very green, 90 degrees, one of the hottest, most humid days we've had yet. Ten families, including twenty-one children, dined outdoors under a bush arbor. Together we cooked four turkeys with dressing, two in my oven because it's larger. All the missionary families except the Currys (home with chicken pox) and several Americans working with the petroleum refinery and U.S. companies in Port Harcourt joined us.

Christmas celebrations here were certainly more relaxing. I'd already done most of my shopping in the States to include in the drums. I ordered magazine subscriptions for the kids and found good books at the SIM (Sudan Interior Mission) bookstore in Port Harcourt, their favorite store. They're getting acquainted with all these wonderful British characters like Paddington Bear and Winnie-the-Pooh. We also found good Nigerian souvenirs for each. I was especially pleased to find an African gourd doll in native costume for Marty -- probably made for tourist trade. Here children don't play with dolls. They usually carry a live one tied on their backs.

Interestingly none of the kids made a Christmas wish list this year. When Lee ventured a suggestion, Marty very maturely said, "Santa might not be able to find that in Nigeria."

Would you believe we even had a real green Christmas tree! Friday Onukafor, Lawyer's cook, said "I know where to find you a tree." And he brought us what they called "pine," a different species, but resembling pine.

The Harold Derr family, who have been working in Ghana for the past year and a half, arrived unexpectedly late last night from Lagos. They are here on visitors' visas waiting for a shipment of food from their supporting congregation. Ghana is now in such political turmoil, they said they average two to three hours a day just looking for food. Fortunately they came at a time for good Christmas leftovers, and I never saw a family enjoy a meal more.

Today we all had lunch "high on the hog" -- Swift's Premium hot dogs, Kraft Miracle Whip, French's mustard, Heinz catsup, Del Monte dills, and Heinz baked beans -- a second holiday feast for us. Thanks to the American companies in Port Harcourt.

Marty received a new bike. Along with the other older kids on campus, she explores the village roads and markets. Free range goats and chickens scatter before them. Dogs dash out to bark, and naked kids come streaming out of the compounds yelling, "Welcome. Welcome. Becca (white person). Becca." One village elder sent a note, "Thank you for allowing your children to visit us." They consider it an honor that we trust them to protect our children. Nigerians love children. Some may recall a time when Nigerians kidnapped children of strangers for their own slaves or pagan rituals.

The harvest field is white. For several weeks Henry and our steward, Monday John, have been market preaching one afternoon a week on the other side of our stream where they speak Efik (our side of the stream is Ibo, Monday is Efik). None of our missionaries had been preaching in that area. Their chief religion is a kind of animism plus the belief that the departed are active in their lives. Others are Catholic, or a mix.

One day Henry, standing near one of the many ju-ju huts (small mud and thatch huts where offerings to spirits are given) asked a man, "What do you think would happen if I were to kick this over?" The man was aghast and said, "You'd die!" Henry said it flitted through his mind that the man might be the means by which he would die should he be tempted to prove him wrong. Of course, he wouldn't have.

How could you expect another to respect your beliefs if you do not respect his? To make a long story short that man is now a leader in one of the three churches they have established in that area.

When pagans are baptized, they are asked to bring out their ju-ju (objects venerated and used as a fetish), and it is burned in the presence of the village to prove they no longer believe in the ju-ju's power. Ju-ju might be anything. Often it's a small carving that has been taken to the native priest for him to invoke a spirit to occupy it through sacrifices and incantations. At one ju-ju burning, the man included an empty penicillin vial he apparently believed had healed him by its power -- true in one way. In the intense heat the vial exploded with a loud bang and sent the onlookers scattering. We've been speculating about what must have gone through their minds then.

Henry is still working on permission to use the old rest house as a temporary dispensary. So far about 300, of the 3000 Nigerian pounds the local people promised by January, has been all they could give -- and that's a large amount for them. Some local leaders who could help are hold-outs for "What's in it for me?" We have the support of the professionals. One, Francis J. Ellah, visited us and said, "What a shame that you have been here all of this time and not be able to do anything!" He made a special trip to Enugu to see the minister of health himself, then told Henry to apply again and it would go through this time. We'll see.

The Nigerian school year ends in December. Just before Christmas we went to the closing Parents' Day program at a local school. We were treated like royalty and given a place of honor with the village chief and school head master. They brought us refreshments of tepid Krola (a kind of cola drink) and cream crackers (a plain British cracker). After an enjoyable program of plays, songs, poems, and dances, they auctioned school crafts such an baskets, embroidery work, etc. and yams grown on the school farm. The money goes to help their school. The governor has decreed that agriculture and domestic sciences be taught in all elementary schools. I bought a lovely hand-embroidered tablecloth for myself and some tree climbing ropes for the boys.

When palm fruit is harvested, the climbers use special ropes around themselves and the tree to gradually work their way upward, sometimes fifty feet or more. The boys have been practicing -- unsuccessfully.

Have a happy year. It will be 1965 when you receive this.

Love,
Dit

January 10, 1965

Dear folks,

Last week I bought fertilizer and began spading up my garden spot. I work out early in the morning to beat the heat, or forget it. Mornings are invigorating, and gardening gives me a reason to be outside. Nights are cool. Dew is so heavy you'd think it had rained during the night. This is dry season which means daily watering, but it also avoids the bugs -- a technique advocated in my books on tropical gardening. Also in rainy season root vegetables rot in the ground.

Heavy tropical rains leach the soil of nutrients. I was trying to explain to the yardman how I wanted him to dig a hole and put in the grass he cut, when to my surprise he answered, "Oh, you mean a compost pit." That's part of their agricultural training in the schools.

We're still on school vacation, and I'm still trying to finish couch covers. While Monday John is also on "holiday," I'm also trying to do the equivalent of a spring housecleaning. Here that includes removing cobwebs, roach egg cases, and lizard eggs from hidden areas, re-waxing the wood furniture, and polishing the Colorcrete floors.

The nurses' house is almost completed, but our visa request for "sister tutors" has been denied. Iris has already sent her barrels, and we hold her keys. Nor has there been any more progress toward permission for a dispensary. The local people simply do not have the money. Either the government must come up with financial aid, or we must find another source.

We have always heard the first six months on the mission field called "the honeymoon period." After that reality sets in. If this is a "honeymoon," I'm not sure how much reality we can take. Twice a week Henry continues to drive about 40 miles to the joint hospital in Umahia (Methodist, Presbyterian, and Anglican). Once a week he works at a Lutheran Hospital. He takes no pay and receives good experience, but he's not accomplishing what he came for.

Nigeria had its first free elections since independence in December. We are still waiting to hear the outcome. There are sharp differences between the large Muslim North and the rest of the country, mainly Christian and animism. We are hopeful that Nigeria can be an example in democracy for other African nations.

Love,
Dit

January 24, 1965

Dear folks,

Our big news this week began last week, January 16, with our trip to the beach. Dr. Preston Manning, Henry's co-worker at Queen Elizabeth Hospital and his family joined us. Dr. Manning, a young surgeon from N.C., took surgery board exams when Henry did. Disappointed in the surgery dept. here, he is preparing to return to the U.S.A. this week.

We all drove to Eket on the Qua Ibo River. After a picnic in the rest house, we bargained with a boatman to take us down the river in a dugout to the Atlantic Beach where we had been with the Bryants (Bight of Biafra) and arranged for him to return in three hours. It was the middle of the day, but we had brought blankets to erect a sunshade with palm fronds. The tide was high and the water very rough with all kinds of debris washing up. Still we were having a great time at the water's edge.

We had been there only a brief time when David, who had been hunting shells in the shallow water, suddenly screamed saying he'd been hit by something. He lay under our shade writhing in pain for the next three hours. There was a small jagged triangular wound at the back of his ankle that bled profusely.

The only medication I had with me was a few baby aspirin I had brought for Lee's earache. I gave him all but it didn't phase him. We had no way to return until the appointed time for the boatmen. All the way home, in the boat and in the car, he lay on the floor rolling and crying with pain. David has never been a complainer. He said it was the worst pain he'd ever had.

Once home we had stronger pain medicine and ice to apply that helped some. The next day his leg began to swell until it was red and swollen to the knee. His temperature rose to 104 and he was delirious. Henry started him on antibiotics. I kept hot packs on his leg around the clock for days. This week he has a draining abscess. For the first time since, his temperature is normal today. He wants to play, but we're keeping him in bed.

This has been a favorite beach for missionaries for years. In fact there were three families from the Qua Ibo church there that same day. We've been making inquiries and have yet to learn of another who has had a similar experience. We have concluded that it must have been a sting ray washed in by the high tide. Henry thinks that all the bleeding he did at the beach may have washed out enough poison to have saved his life. Rather than write about this last week, we decided it was better to wait until we were sure he was well on the road to recovery.

David Bryant, the same age but taller than Lee, received a new 16-inch bike. Thursday, Lee practically took it away from him. I never saw such determination to conquer anything in my life. Lee wasn't tall enough to sit on the seat nor could he reach the hand brakes, but that didn't stop him. He was on it before breakfast. As Rees said he "saluted" his meals. In the heat of the day he was still working away with a red face and the sweat pouring off. I was so concerned that I held him down awhile to force him to rest, but he kicked and screamed the whole time. Since Henry had to go to Aba, he brought back ice to make ice cream. I guess that saved him. It was the only thing for which he would stop and eat. Before the day was over he was riding so well that the next day, Friday, he rode it to the Onicha Ngwa market about a mile away. How's that for a four-year-old's determination? By

Saturday, Henry felt so sorry for David Bryant because Lee had taken over his bike, that he bought Lee a new bike. Now Lee is so proud he can ride with the "big kids." Today he is still madly peddling up and down the walk.

He's been on a "teach me to read" kick, spurning kindergarten. With his kind of determination, it shouldn't be a problem. He watches me teach the others and he's not going to be left out of anything. I don't have the right books for him, but I showed him a few words -- and he doesn't forget.

Besides the couch covers and drapes, I've been sewing shifts, "tent dresses," for Marty and myself. For this heat I need dresses that hit my body only at the shoulders -- no belts, sleeves, or collars -- and of a material heavy enough to not need a slip. Forget appearance, "survival" is the word in this heat. I sit with arms and legs extended straight out. Two skin surfaces touching stick together.

I dug up a sizeable garden spot by hand and have planted spinach, okra, and popcorn (Paul's request) and made seed beds starting tomato. eggplant, and cabbage. The Nigerians come by to watch and say "Jesike." The Ibo word "ike" means "power," so it's something like "more power to you." I think they're not expecting white women to dig in the ground like theirs. The big difference is that I'm not dependent on gardening for my livelihood, but it's a kind of experiment to see what can be done and good exercise. Hank is so interested, I've given him the job of watering.

The Bible School reopened this week for a new school year so my steward is back in school, working for me part time. In addition to our school and all my other projects, I will now pick up the work he doesn't have time for and serve as school nurse. I don't usually do much more for students than give out aspirin and malaria pills. No matter what the problem, malaria pills will always make them feel better.

Monday John is a real jewel. He has such a cheerful disposition our whole family loves him. It's a joy to have him working and singing around the house. His dedication to the Lord's work is an example of what we hope to accomplish here. When the kids are out of sorts, he can always make them laugh with his antics, funny faces, and songs, even standing on his head. He can work faster then any Nigerian I have seen. He's the top of the class in the Bible College. In addition to his native Efik, he speaks fluent English and some Ibo, so he's both an excellent preacher and interpreter.

He understands American idioms and the differences in the British and American English. Americans have redefined many words such as "mad" and "wonderful," which are still used in their original sense here. He says, "I know when the Americans say 'wonderful' it means something different." Originally "wonderful" (full of wonder) and "awful" (full of awe) had essentially the same meaning, but we now use one to imply good and the other to mean bad. I'll have to admit it startled me the first time I told a Nigerian someone had died and watched him snap his fingers exclaiming, "Wonderful! Wonderful!"

Our school year began before I had time to finish all my couch covers so I gave the job to a local tailor who was also a preacher. When Henry preached at his church I noticed that his daughter was wearing a dress made from my material. The cloth was so unusual, I'd found it only in Port Harcourt, and I'd bought it all. It had to have been mine. I was so miserable thinking of him as a thief that I had no choice but to ask him about it. He told me that it was the Nigerian custom that the scraps belonged to the tailor. I told him that it was not the American custom, and with scraps that big I could have used them myself. I asked him to please return all scraps, large or small, in the future and he agreed. So I left feeling better having gone to him.

Our dry season brings the Harmattan winds full of fine reddish dust from the Sahara, and "camel dung" Henry adds. I always know it's coming before we see it because Henry develops asthma. You see the dust. You feel the dust. You taste the dust. The atmosphere becomes hazy. Sunsets turn crimson. And the tropical moon, always exquisite, reddens. A film of fine dust covers everything and penetrates every crack!

Love,
Dit

January 31, 1965

Dear folks,

It is Sunday morning. Paul has gone on a preaching trip with his dad. David had another abscess come up near the site of the first so he is still on bed rest with hot packs, but improving. Hank had 102 to 103 fever the past few days, but is responding to antimalarials. As a whole our family has never had a healthier winter, and he's the first with malaria. As time goes by I have more and more admiration for the missionaries who came before modern drugs. Their plight has been immortalized in the jingle:

> Beware and take care of the Bight of Benin
> Where few come out though many go in.

(British rhyme the final syllables with an "een" sound.)

It is very common to hear the sounds of drums and dancing at night (if a full moon, all night) -- so common, in fact, I can sleep through it like the ticking of a clock. But today I awoke to very loud drumming. My workers tell me the drums are announcing time to go work in the fields. We are surrounded by SDA's (Seventh Day Adventists) and they seem to take delight in letting us know they work on Sundays.

Finally it seems some progress is being made toward a clinic. This week the D.O. (District Officer) came to dinner and was enthusiastic for the work. He says he will make a trip to Enugu to see the Minister of Health on our behalf tomorrow. Last evening we entertained the S.M.O. (Senior Medical Officer) of the Aba district. He left saying he would write a letter to the minister on our behalf the same night. So much is accomplished here by knowing the right people.

Both felt that the best way to begin was with an out-patient clinic in the old rest house, but that we could not rely on local funds, though people would probably give more if they saw something being done. No American church has yet been interested in giving toward a medical work here. Though they did not feel they could assume that responsibility, the West End elders did not discourage us from trying other sources. Dr. George Benson and Dr. Adrian Formby (Patti Bryant's uncle) of Searcy have requested permission to raise funds for a clinic.

The nurses' house has been completed and is now being painted. Henry received a copy of the letter written to Lagos Immigration by the S.M.O. requesting that the nurses be allowed to enter. Waiting is "the name of the game." Brother Akandu, BTC headmaster, continues to gently admonish Henry, "Let us exercise patience."

My tomatoes, okra, and corn came up with Hank's faithful watering -- no more rains.

We just received a box George had mailed us in Sept. exempt from customs because some books were included. It also had a sink drainboard which made my steward very happy because air drying saves his time and me happy because it's more sanitary than dishtowels.

Love,
Dit

February 14, 1965

Dear folks,

David is so much better he wants to be up more than we allow. His accident was a month ago, but he still had draining abcesses. We have learned from natives that sting rays are not uncommon in that area. In fact they catch them there for food.

We have just finished a very inspirational week with Brother J.P. Sanders, who has been working in Germany with the Pepperdine University extension. He left Saturday saying that his association with the missionaries and students here has made this one of the most outstanding weeks of his life. In the same way he left us with much food for thought, and his visit had a profound effect on the students. Each family enjoyed hosting him to become better acquainted.

I'd heard that a few days of rain in the middle of dry season could be possible. This was the chosen week! For two days the thunder cracked and the rains poured. The arbor our workers had built as a sunshade for an outdoor lectureship was useless in the torrents. Brother Sanders commented, "If this is your dry season, I'm glad I didn't come during the wet one."

I am now using tomatoes from my own vines and the okra is doing well, but other things are not. I found "acclimatized" corn seed to replace mine. Yesterday Paul and I planted watermelon as an experiment. My tropical gardening books say lettuce should be planted in seed beds with sterilized soil then transplanted or the ants will eat the seeds before they can germinate. The grass has been so shriveled and brown we could see the bare ground riddled with ant holes. I marvel that there is enough dirt between to hold land together.

We received word from the Derrs that they had returned safely to Ghana, but their situation there is impossible. The nation is so bankrupt that their income cannot meet the 10% sales tax imposed.

They had hoped that the food they received while here would last them until they could transfer elsewhere. They are interested in Nigeria, but we have not yet been able to increase our quota. Rees and Phil Dunn left this morning for Lagos to make another attempt to get it increased.

Since I last wrote, Henry and all the boys have had bouts with malaria, flu-like symptoms, and recovered. Guess which is the "weaker sex!"

Lee is reading so well at age four and a half he's halfway through Hank's first book though I have spent very little time with him.

We have just been informed by the post office that they are holding six boxes for us and customs will be $45 -- a considerable expense on our present income. We have no idea yet who sent them or what they contain. If anyone wants to send us gifts, please suggest that they send the money for customs as well.

Love,
Dit

February 28, 1965

Dear folks,

"The best part of Christmas in Nigeria is that it lasts for months." Such was Marty's statement last week when we brought home the boxes from the post office. The second Christmas, so unexpected, was even more exciting than the first and demanded another school holiday. A congregation where Henry had preached sent three boxes of toys; the VA hospital where he had worked sent a fruit cake; and Flora sent a set of biographies. There's still one large box from another church being held because it has no slip stating the value of the contents. I'm embarrassed to write them for an invoice for their gifts; but it's either that or we don't get them. New toys and books make the rounds of all the families, so we have a very excited bunch of kids on campus now.

This week we were delighted to have as our guest, Dr. Benjamin Wilson of Vanderbilt, here working on a nutrition study the National Institute of Health is doing in connection with the University of Ibadan. He collected food samples from the market and observed our workers prepare their "chop" and toss the garri balls down their throats. He's also been studying a mold on peanuts. He attends church at Hillsboro with Henry's mother so she'll be happy for a direct report.

One day he made the trip to Umuahia with Henry flying down village roads that look more like foot paths, scattering chickens and goats all directions. He returned saying, "If you want the thrill of a lifetime, just take a ride down the bush roads with Henry." I hope he doesn't report that part to her.

The trip to Lagos Immigration was a success! Our visa quota has been raised from 11 to 22, and we can expect the nurses soon. Progress toward a clinic seems hemmed in by unexpected legalities at every turn. Villages have unregulated midwives and bone-setters, hastily trained dispensers, and "witch doctors" (they prefer the term "native doctors"), but laws governing the practice of physicians are more stringent than in America.

The political situation is quiet now. Referring to Ghana, the Nigerian president recently said, "If independence means the substitution of indigenous tyranny for alien rule, then the government has betrayed the people."

Temperature-wise this past week has been an exhausting one. Lee broke out in a heat rash, and my hair stays stuck to my head. A sausage bug just crossed the table in front of me with David close behind eager for an addition to his collection. He'd read about them before coming and staked his claim. The locals are very happy for this new addition to their diet. Monday says they also cut open dead palm trees to eat the grubs, about the size of an adult finger. I asked, "How do you cook them?" And he replied, "Just like a hot dog, Madam."

Finally, six weeks since the beach accident, Henry told David he could ride a bike tomorrow. He's counting the hours. He had such a hole where the tissues sloughed that Henry, afraid of osteomyelitis, took him to be x-rayed at Umuahia, but there was no evidence of infection.

We have moved our Sunday evening services up to 4 P.M. to accommodate the people who come from Port Harcourt, so I'm now writing afterward. Today Henry went to a congregation where he had not been before and returned with a pineapple, eggs, and six stalks of bananas. Dry season makes the most wonderfully sweet pineapple. I never liked pineapple before coming here. Now I eat till my mouth is sore. Oranges were in season at five for a penny, but now they are a penny each -- "Penny-penny" they say.

My okra was doing beautifully till the bugs attacked it. Before I could get to town to find some kind of insecticide, they had finished it off. The tomatoes are healthy. The corn is a foot high. Lettuce, cabbage, collards, eggplant, and the watermelon are up.

The Beckloffs took us to a private swimming hole on the Ag farm, and now we've been twice. Paul and Marty taught Henry how to float on his back -- a great achievement for one so afraid of water he'd scream he was drowning if his toenails couldn't scratch the sand. Perhaps seeing that his children had become accomplished swimmers was too much for him.

Ever since Lee took off on a bike, I decided perhaps I could master one too. I practice on the tennis court when I think no one is looking and use the kid's bike so my feet can easily touch the ground if necessary. Even so I've had some "bang-up" practices.

Bryants have a TV now and the older kids are there watching American reruns. Lee is begging me to play a game with him and so I will.

Love,
Dit

March 7, 1965

Dear folks,

Just as I'm ready to write the kids have dashed home from Sunday night reruns at the Bryants, barely ten minutes before the lights will go out. That means I'll be hovering over a hot candle; and although the flame is small, it will be the only light. I'll be swatting bugs, blinking bugs, and spitting bugs.

But then you'd be surprised all our screens do keep out! In this land of insect overpopulation, Americans are the only ones who insist on screens. Living in a British house at Queen Elizabeth Hospital, Dr. Manning's wife said every night she had to choose between bugs and cross-ventilation. The anti-screen people contend that screens cut off air and have wood shutters.

Henry bought a radio, a record player and Dr. Manning's big speaker. I'm quite content to be TV free. I did manage to pack our whole set of Columbia classics in those round drums in such a way that none were broken or warped through months in the hot hold of a ship.

The change to a 4 p.m. worship services to accommodate the visitors also avoids all the night bugs attracted to the only electric lights in miles. The light directly above the preacher's stand was their favorite. One Sunday night before the change, Doug stood up to preach, cleared his throat deeply, then walked to the window to spit. I knew we were informal, but this! Later he told us that just as he opened his mouth to speak, a bug went down.

No preaching trips for Henry today. He's been in bed all day with his second attack of malaria within the month and "weak as water." He's decided that for his size he should double the dose of malaria prophylaxis.

Daily temperatures of 90 to 95 degree wouldn't be so miserable if the humidity were not the same. We no longer have the shield of rain clouds -- only the brassy tropical sun. Even the beds are so hot at night I crawl onto the cool bare concrete floor for a few hours sleep. We painted our walls a cool blue and Henry found a snow scene to hang. Sometimes Doug even turns on the generator in the heat of the day to run the ceiling fans. Then we can sit under the fan and gaze at the snow.

The children have stuck to their school work in spite of the heat. Lee is reading in the second preprimer, so he will read aloud to himself while I work with the others. Hank reads well for first grade, but has an eye coordination problem. We have to cover the line he's not reading with a card to train his eyes, or he skips words and lines and the story doesn't make sense to him. David has such a keen, analytical mind he compensates well for his dyslexia -- when he can keep his mind on the subject. Marty breezes through every lesson and has fallen in love with poetry. She wants to make every required composition into a poem. Paul is happy that the shorter school hours allows time for books of his own choosing. A digger for facts, he's been reading through the encyclopedias donated by World Book.

Trips to Enugu for a dispensary seem unending. Sometimes the proper official is "not on seat today." Sometimes Henry is told he must do some insignificant thing they hadn't required before. Are they so new at the job they are afraid to act with authority? Do they really want to do what is best, but aren't sure how? Do they hope for a "service fee" under the table? Are they just being certain that we understand that they are the ones in charge? We really haven't been able to figure it all out. In the meantime people are dying around us for lack of care.

When Henry took his well designed plans, that would have found approval in America, they found some little thing or two that was not exactly like their model plans and sent him away. Friday he returned with the revisions. Meanwhile officials had changed, but he came home more hopeful.

I've been doing the finishing touches for the nurses' house -- making curtain for shades, getting furniture made and waxed to prevent mold, etc. In our discussions about who could do their housework, Charla suggested Mark Apollos, an apprentice under her cook Friday Onukafor. Mark has been honest, likable, and capable. Though illiterate, he memorizes the recipes.

The possibility was brought up that someone might wonder about our having a single young Nigerian man working for the single nurses. It was decided that if anyone should ask, we'd just have to let them know this is not America. Charla will have Friday concentrate on training Mark to be ready when they arrive; and with only the two, one worker should be enough.

The children have been so interested in our garden that we all get out to dig, plant, and water during the brief cool of the day. They are especially interested in the corn and watermelon. To Nigerians it's a waste to pick "green cobs," so we have had a hard time finding corn here as tender as we like it. They eat it hard, roasted over charcoal.

I have the same problem trying to get a tender chicken. I asked the poultry farm manager if he had any for sale, and he said, "Not yet. Wait a few more months." When I asked, "How old are they now?" He answered, "Seven months." That's why we need pressure cookers.

Our washerman, a Christian, wanted time off because his father was giving a feast in honor of his grandmother who died 10 years ago. They will be drumming and dancing all night. It is customary here to honor deceased ancestors on an important death anniversary, apparently to keep their spirit happy so they won't do anything bad. Family and village pressures are so strong it is hard for any Christian not to go along. Monday night -- Henry was much better today and hopes to work tomorrow, but David came down with his second attack of malaria in a month. Don't expect to hear from us for at least two weeks. We'll be heading for the hills -- Obudu Ranch in the Cameroonian foothills -- altitude about one mile.

Love,
Dit

March 30, 1965

Dear folks,

Obudu exceeded our expectations, even after hearing Bryants' enthusiastic report of their time there. The government operates a catering resthouse, an experimental farm, and a cattle ranch on about 30 square miles of rolling hills near the Cameroonian border. With an elevation of a mile, it was so cool that it was hard to believe we were still in Nigeria. They keep several thousand head of Fulani cattle (named for the tribal herdsmen), a zebu-type with Texas-sized longhorns. They had two new Devon bulls imported from England to develop a beefy breed that could survive in the tropics. It's still very much the dry season. Returning to the rest house from our long daily hikes, we sang "The camels are coming," then downed water by the pitcherful. Saddle horses (some so slow they could hardly qualify for the name) and a few burros were fun. Marty, especially, loves anything that resembles a horse.

Our favorite spot was a water hole fed by two waterfalls, one below the other. Shaded by a heavy canopy of trees and vines, the water was refreshingly cold for swimming. The banks were covered with moss and native orchids. I wouldn't have been surprised to see Tarzan come swinging out at any moment.

A "catering rest house" provides lodging and meals at a flat rate. From their experimental gardens we had an abundance of fresh vegetables. The kids had heard that real milk was available and drank their fill. Fresh strawberries was another anticipated treat, but to their disappointment "strawberries and cream" translated into a few berries immersed in a bowl of Bird's custard, a tasteless sauce the British love to pour over most desserts.

Meals were cooked and served in a proper British fashion. Stewards brought the food to our table in large bowls and served our plates using two implements. Separate courses from soup to cheese and coffee (following dessert) were very formal served on a dish on a dish on a dish. I made certain I kept my fork in my right hand so everyone would know I was American.

It was a real put down for the younger three when they learned that children under ten do not eat evening meals with parents. They were not too happy with beans or spaghetti on toast at 6 p.m. while Paul and Marty could have potatoes and steak with us at 8:00. I couldn't resist smuggling them a bit.

My favorite after dinner pastime was Scrabble with an international crowd. I was introduced not only to a new Oxford vocabulary, but also to a new alphabet, e.g. "zed" for "zee."

The weather seemed even more uncomfortable on our return, but we were greeted with such good news we could put it all behind us. We turned out en masse to welcome Iris Hays last Wed. (March 24). Nancy Petty will be coming April 7. Today Iris went with Henry to Umuahia. He is so happy! He finally feels like a doctor with his own nurse.

A few nights ago we were almost shaken out of bed by intermittent blasting. The next day our workers told us that the native doctor was opening a new place of business and he was clearing the place of evil spirits. The native doctor is always the most prosperous in any village. Many villages have no one else to treat their ills. A "witch doctor" can open a place whenever or wherever he wishes, and Henry has spent eight months working hard for permission to open a modern out-patient clinic.

At each visit to the Ministry of Health they look at his plans with, "Yes. Yes. This is good." Then he leaves and waits. When there has been no action, he returns to find they have tucked the plans away in some bottom drawer and have to search for them. They take another look, make another minor suggestion, and send him away. The whole process is repeated again and again -- revising, visiting, and waiting -- revising, visiting, and waiting.

My corn is now four feet high and watermelon vines six feet long. Most of my American varieties are not doing well. I plan to get my next seeds from the Ag farm where they are tested for the tropics.

March 31 -- Henry has been ill again, apparently malaria. He belittles my regimen of insect repellent every night, but one of us has to stay well. One evening when Rees had come to the house to see Henry on business, he watched me lather every exposed inch with repellent then asked, "Does she do that every night?" To Henry's affirmative, Rees answered, "I like for Patti to smell a little better than that!"

Love,
Dit

May 11, 1965

Dear folks,

First, all are well except Hank.
That little monkey, jumpin' on the bed
bounced on the floor and broke his head.
Doctor Daddy taped his nose, and then he said,
"Don't ever let me catch you jumpin' on the bed!"

After striking his head on bare concrete, Hank can be thankful he'll have only a few days of adhesive tape ("plaster") across his nose.

Now, the GOOD NEWS! We finally have the approval to convert the old Ndiakata rest house into a clinic! It might never have come about had not the Nigerian manager of the Aba TV station visited us then put his influence behind the application. He had studied with RCA in New York and while there married an American. He understood what could and should be done for his people.

On his own initiative he went to Enugu and literally walked the necessary papers from one office to the next. He told us that he stood at each official's desk until he was told what the next step would be. Then he hand-carried the papers to that place and waited until he saw it done. He proceeded thus from office to office, never allowing the request to be "filed" in a bottom drawer. When they finally ran out of delaying tactics, the request was granted. It takes a Nigerian to understand how Nigeria moves.

Henry swung into high gear with carpenters, plumbers, and masons working away on renovations. With his typical optimism he hopes to complete it all by next week except the well -- and he has been getting estimates on that.

In the meantime the nurses, Iris and Nancy, accompany him on his medical trips. One day Henry introduced me as his wife when a Nigerian he had met on one of these trips paid us a visit. When the man nonchalantly questioned, "Now, this is not the wife I saw you with the other day?" Henry hastened to explain. While we kid Henry about his three wives, I wonder how many others they've credited with multiple wives.

For the days Iris and Nancy don't go with Henry, they teach women's health and Bible classes in the surrounding villages. Henry has hired as interpreters Comfort and Rhoda, two Nigerians with some practical nurse experience who speak English well. People welcome them with so many dashes -- fruit, eggs, chickens, and even a live goat -- that the two can't eat it all. So the rest of us are happy to help them.

My corn crop is "finished" (Nigerian for "used up") -- succulent while it lasted. Now local corn is coming into season, and Tom knows how to find the best "green cobs." Our watermelons made beautiful vines, but when the fruit was about a foot long they suddenly turned black. I'm learning about the "melon fly." The larva develops inside them from eggs laid in the fruit's early formation. There is less problem with the fly if the watermelon is planted at the beginning of dry season. There are no failures in gardening -- just lessons. And there is always another year.

Today a man gave us some fresh local cashews, which our cook knew how to handle, The plant is related to our poison ivy and the inner shell has an oil that can blister the skin. Roasting them makes the outer shell burst and releases the oil. Like poison ivy caught in a wood fire, the fumes can be irritating also. Enough heat destroys the poison. Later the inner shells are broken open by hand and the kernel roasted again. Delicious -- but what a laborious process! Roasted cashews sell for a penny a small bag in Aba. Now I'll have a new appreciation when I pop one in my mouth.

Hank turned seven on April 30 so we had everyone over for ice cream. With twelve kids on campus there's always a party.

The Lawyer family plan to return to America next week leaving a vacancy that no one else can really fill. They have been working here for four years with only a six months leave between tours, and they spent a lot of that reporting and fund raising.

For the summer we are expecting John and Donna Morgan of Nashville. He is a medical student from Vanderbilt, sponsored by a Smith, Kline,& French, a pharmaceutical company, and Donna is an elementary teacher in the Nashville. Both will be real assets here.

We've begun Ibo language lessons. It's my first experience with a non-Indo-European language. One word can have many different meanings depending on the tone and usage. I'm almost too afraid to open my mouth, wondering what I am really saying. Of course such a minor detail never deterred Henry. Driving to Aba recently he passed a lady he thought he recognized and yelled "Jairo, bico." Not until she had whirled in astonishment, almost catapulting her huge head load, did he realize that instead of greeting her, he'd just said what he'd been saying all morning to patients -- "Lie down, please."

Love,
Dit

May 25, 1965

Dear folks,

Rainy season usually begins in April when the winds shift from bringing us the Sahara dust of the north to the Atlantic rains of the east. The early rains came with a fierce electrical display and hard driving winds. They sweep so straight across the land that we call them "horizontal rains." Usually it is in the evening that we find ourselves mopping up an indoor flood on the eastern side of our house -- no matter how tightly we close our louvered glass windows.

One evening a few days after the rains really began, I thought I heard hail hitting our windows. Instead it was a hail of "white ants," an African termite, attracted to our electric lights. The windows were so covered they cut off our ventilation. In spite of closed windows and screens, they are so persistent that hundreds made it inside our house. There they mate and lose their wings. The next morning Monday John came through with a pan of water sprinkling the tiny transparent wings so he could sweep them up into piles. I read that one queen can lay between 3000 and 5000 eggs a day. Multiplying that by the number that invaded our house alone is as staggering as the national debt.

Because Marty wanted to celebrate her eleventh birthday before Shauna left, Shauna and Sara Jo had a birthday dinner with us then spent the night with her. She has been wanting a Nigerian dress, so I had one made of dark green cloth with yellow roosters and "Federation of Nigeria" and "Independence 1960" printed on it in dark red. The cloth, printed in Nigeria, is a local favorite now. The dress is also a favorite style -- a blouse with a peplum and a straight piece of fabric that extends to the floor when wrapped at the waist as you might a bath towel. She's so proud of it.

The nurses' gift was a dugout ride poled down the Qua Ibo River. Like a scene from the *African Queen*, the stillness was overwhelming. The only sounds were the dipping of the poles into the water and strange noises from the thick vegetation and vines **overhanging the banks. The only signs of civilization were the** occasional fish traps.

For dental care here we depend on an American dentist at the Baptist Clinic in Enugu. Last week Marty had a baby tooth pulled with a cavity deep enough to hurt. Henry also had one pulled, unfortunately not a baby tooth. There are said to be 36 dentists in all of Nigeria (population **approx. 1 million**). As a whole the Nigerians in our area appear to have good teeth. They eat very few sweets and it is very common to see them going around with a chewing stick in their mouths working on their teeth. The sticks are made of a wood that softens into a kind of brush when moistened in the mouth. In fact different tribes have different kinds of wood that each insists is best. Sometimes the handles even have fancy carvings.

In addition to being principal of the Bible Training School, Doug kept everything on campus in good working condition for us. The night after he left our generator "died." Tonight we have the "bush lamps" (kerosene lanterns) and the Tilley lamps (kerosene pressure lamps) going, waiting for generator repairs. Poor Rees is left to deal with it all now.

Love,
Dit

June 5, 1965

Dear folks,

Yesterday was a day to celebrate! My first ripe watermelon! I even have a photo to prove it. As far as I know I've been the first in this area to successfully grow one though many have tried. In fact so many ripened we had watermelon daily for about a week. Our workers had never seen anything like them. They shook their heads and snapped their fingers in amazement and amusement, but most didn't care for the taste.

I am now harvesting lettuce (Bibb seems to do best) and a second crop of corn and collards. The collards were an inspiration from the black American wife of the Aba TV station manager. From the South via New York City, she was having success and told me, "If there was a black person living in the Empire State building, he would have collard greens growing on top." Henry has always teased me about my "brown thumb," but I'd warned him he would live to eat those words some day.

I've been getting the "Lawyer house" ready for John and Donna Morgan, who are scheduled to arrive in four days -- waxing floors, washing curtains, painting walls, etc. Henry insists on it having special attention because he's convinced that the secret to keeping missionaries on the field is keeping the wives happy.

We are winding up our school year with Calvert home study. Donna has said she would like to teach our younger children, so every day has been like anticipating Christmas for Hank and Lee -- "How long now before my new teacher comes?"

Converting the old rest house into a clinic, like everything else, takes more time than we had thought. We're learning to expect the unexpected. A torrential downpour caved in a septic tank almost completed. That one thing alone set the work back a week. Money is now coming in from interested individuals, some not even members of the church.

All is not work with no play. Sunday evening we took the family to see *Ben Hur* at the Hotel Presidential in Port Harcourt, about an hour's drive away. We felt perfectly safe coming home around midnight (Note: This would not be true in present day Nigeria.) Occasionally we go to the Aba theater where the ads are more entertaining than the movies and the kids go around imitating them for days -- "Guiness is gooood for you."

For Sara Jo's tenth birthday the Bryants took all the kids swimming in the Olympic-sized pool at the Shell Oil Compound, Port Harcourt, then treated them to hamburgers and french fries ("chips") -- a real taste of home! The Shell compound is a special enclave designed to keep the foreign workers (mostly British and Dutch) happy, but it took a Texas oilman to go back into the kitchen and say, "Let me show you how to make a real hamburger."

Hank's nose is straight, but now he's sporting a splint on his right arm. The kids were standing around the open garbage pit just looking in when Becki Bryant with the impulsiveness of a 3-year-old suddenly gave him a shove. Lee was showing off for Cindi Lawyer before she left and ended up with a black eye and three stitches above it from the fall. How did missionary families ever manage without a built-in doctor!

But those were not the worst. The boys have been making bows and using the sharpened ribs of palm fronds for arrows. I should have thought ahead, but it would never have occurred to me that David might try the William Tell thing with an orange on Lee's head. I was at the kitchen window when I heard the scream. Looking up I saw Lee running from behind Bryant's house with an arrow protruding from his face. I almost fainted. It appeared to be in his eye, but as it turned out the arrow was about an inch below it. How do kids ever reach adulthood!

Our world news comes to us via radio and special editions of *Time* and *Life* -- a very different perspective from this side. It's enough to make me wonder if I ever want to return to America. Here we've experienced no black/white prejudice, but the black/black prejudice exceeds anything I ever heard of in America. The African tribes were warring among themselves killing, torturing, kidnapping, and enslaving long before white people saw these shores. Centuries-old tribal hatreds run deep. One of the greatest testimonies to the power of the Gospel has been seeing these men from enemy tribes studying Bible together in our schools.

When an Efik Judge, the Honorable A.E. Bassey of Ikot Ekpene, paid us a welcoming call in Iboland, he said that the missionaries were given this land because it had been a battleground between the two tribes and people were afraid of the spirits. He said they were hopeful that a Bible College would bring peace. He added, "In the past I would have been afraid to go down this road (referring to the village road that runs through our compound) in the daytime, but now I would not be afraid to sleep in the middle of the road at night."

I like to help the food sellers who come to our door with vegetables, beef, and fish. One day a man had both purple and green eggplants. Having never seen a green one, I wondered if it was unripe or a new variety. I beckoned to my steward, "Monday, why is one eggplant green and the other purple?" Throwing back his head, he laughed heartily and answered, " I don't know, Madam. Why are some of us black and some of us white?" And that very well characterizes the attitude I've experienced here.

In fact everything we do here seems to be deeply appreciated. Recently I showed a preacher supporting six children on $6/mo. plus a little tailoring how to make peanut butter. "Ground nuts" (peanuts) are 7 cups/shilling (about 14 cents) in the market. I tried to explain iron-deficiency anemia and the nutritional value of peanuts. He was eager go home and make peanut butter for his family saying, "Oh, if we only knew about foods they way you do." Most deficiencies we see are not from the lack of good food available but from poor food habits and ignorance about nutrition.

Sometimes it frightens me the way they attach so much importance to all I say for fear I'll say the wrong thing. A former missionary once said they made her feel like a combination of Marilyn Monroe and Mamie Eisenhower.

Love,
Dit

Note: One of our joys has been seeing the children assume responsibility for what they can do. Marty wrote her grandmother Farrar on June 8:

"Guess what? My friend Sara and I want to teach Bible so we are going to have a weekly Bible class. We're having the first one this afternoon and the lesson is on Adam and Eve. This class is for the small American children on the compound. Hank also loves to listen to the Bible. Sometimes he comes to me and asks me to read the Bible to him. I helped him learn the 23rd Psalm."

(In the following weeks Sara and Marty conducted their weekly afternoon Bible classes for the preschool children on campus with as much careful preparation as any adult and made excellent use of visual aids. The younger children really looked forward to their class.)

June 16, 1965

Dear folks.

Like son, like father! Sporting the latest in father/son outfits are our two Henrys, both with right arms in casts. X-rays showed a definite fracture of Hank's forearm. Henry's came as a result of a fall on the tennis court. He says he wishes he could think up a more exotic reason to report. Following a welcoming dinner for the Morgans, we had tennis matches. Henry and a Nigerian teacher were champs, but in the process he fell. No fracture showed on his x-ray, but by the symptoms he believes he may have fractured the small bone in the wrist that controls the thumb, and he says that doesn't always show. They put his arm in a cast for two weeks.

Henry has been so excited to have another doctor (well, almost a doctor) and was looking forward to teaching John Morgan surgery that he might not have the opportunity to do in America as a senior medical student. I don't know which doctor is the most disappointed. Donna is doing double duty as a secretary for Henry, who can't use his right hand just now, as well as teaching Hank and Lee.

The old rest house has the same three buildings that Bill and Gerry Nicks lived in when they came to Iboland in 1957. We are remodeling them into examining rooms, a lab, a pharmacy, an office and restrooms. The nurses have been busy selecting the equipment, getting curtains made for the examining rooms, planning training courses, etc. Water is our biggest problem. Since it may be months before we can procure a driller or the $3000 needed, we decided to buy a petrol pump and install it at the stream.

Hundreds have been applying for the few clinic jobs. The nurses have been designing a test based on intelligence and reasoning ability rather than facts that they may have memorized as a way to select those most trainable. They've been warned that their test must be kept securely locked.

Paul Dillingham from Reed Ave. congregation, Nashville, arrived to spend a month with Beckloffs. He came with an acute bronchitis that Henry has been treating. One of the major reasons for selecting this site was to be of medical service to missionaries.

For one of her Scout badges, I took Marty to meet with the Girl Guides (the British name) at Port Harcourt. She spent the afternoon learning first aid with them. For a cycling badge Iris Hays took the girls on an all day cycling trip. After having had classes in all the villages, she is familiar with the roads. It really has been great for our kids, especially the girls, to have the nurses here -- in fact, a real boost for us all.

Rainy season is fully here! With clouds shielding the sun, the Nigerians complain of the cold -- one morning as low as 55 F. As they shiver and pull their wrappers around them, I feel alive once more!

Love,
Dit

July 6, 1965

Dear folks,

Henry's cast is off. He had said that sometimes a break in the wrist may not be visible on the first film, then shows up later. A second x-ray also showed no break. It was probably a very bad sprain, but it hurt no less. Hank will wear his cast two more weeks.

The heavy rains do not seem to hinder any phase of life as they might in America. Right now, through a torrential downpour, I see a bus at the school loading the students to go to Ukpom Bible College for a "football" (soccer) match. Rees has taken advantage of the rains to hire a nursery to set out fruit trees and flowering shrubs on the campus. I now have a gardenia and a camellia along with my bougainvillaea, hibiscus, and frangipani.

The clinic is so near completion we are planning opening ceremonies for "Nigerian Christian Hospital, Stage I." When Henry and Marty had dental appointments in Enugu last week, he took his revised hospital plans to the Minister of Health. So we're playing the waiting game now for Stage II.

Sunday the children and I accompanied Henry on his preaching trip. Afterward we all went to a stream where the interpreter baptized four. Streams are so shallow here that the baptisms are done from a sitting position. In the afternoon Monday baptized a teacher from a Catholic school who had been studying with him. Before the baptism Henry asked him if he realized this would mean the end of his job, and he answered that he believed he had found the truth and had no other choice. Sure enough, on Monday morning the school manager called him in and asked if the reports he had heard were true. Jobs are so "dear" it took a lot of faith for him to leave one for his convictions. That kind of faith is not really unusual here.

Why have the Africans as a whole been more responsive to Christianity than people of Western cultures? We have always known that religion has more appeal to the poor and disadvantaged because they recognize their need, but there is more. I've been doing a lot of reading and questioning, searching for the answer.

While we often feel compelled to categorize, classify, and compartmentalize every part of life, the African sees the whole as a spiritual experience. Nigerians often attribute physical problems to a spiritual source and believe they have offended some vengeful spirit though they may not know the offence. That remains for the native doctor ("witch doctor") to tell them and may cost them considerable cash and possibly an animal sacrifice.

Their belief in a benevolent Supreme Being over all other spirits was verified by their language spoken long before missionaries arrived -- "Chineke," the Creator, or "Chukwu," the Great God. This God looks with favor on mankind and brings good his way, yet he is also the just punisher of wrongdoing.

"Ekwensu," translated Devil, is the author of all evil, opposed to Chineke and associated with many evil spirits, yet none can do more than God will allow. I have yet to hear an Ibo question the New Testament demons that we have struggled to explain. Neither is the existence of a future life ever argued.

Murder, thievery, adultery and lying are recognized as crimes, but to be found out is often considered more shameful than the act itself. Committed against a village brother or friendly neighbor they are very serious while they may be winked at if against an outsider.

While we see many little "ju-ju" huts with carvings and offerings, we cannot say they "bow down to wood and stone." Any object that appeals to person may become his fetish, or "ju-ju," after a qualified intermediary has consecrated it through what he deems proper sacrifices or incantations to invoke a spirit to live in the object. It is to the spirit residing in the "wood and stone" to which the man appeals.

Another reason I think they understand the Bible better is because their way of life is so similar to that of Bible times. They know about planting seeds and harvesting, lighting candles, rolling up sleeping mats, etc. There is also so much similarity in their social customs -- bride prices, inheriting a brother's wife, paid funeral lamenters, patriarchal family system, special honor and duties of the first-born son, respect for age, etc. Besides animal sacrifices, native Ibo religious rituals of the past resembled Israelite practices in such things as purification ceremonies, cleansing of a house, food and drink offerings, special significance in trees, naming ceremonies, harvest thanksgiving ceremonies, "scape-goats," circumcision on the eighth day, and many others.

Only a blood sacrifice was made for sins. Now sacrifices are usually a chicken or a goat. In years past, before the British outlawed it, a human sacrifice was considered the last appeal if animal sacrifices did not bring the desired result. Even those who no longer believe in sacrifices have seen and heard enough from those who did to understand their significance. When the Ibo hears how Chineke gave his only son to be our sin-bearer, he appreciates it in a way that we may not.

Contrary to popular rumor, the native African was never "running happily through the jungle picking coconuts" before the white man came. His life was burdened from birth to death with tabus and fears. It was the fear that he would offend some spirit, not knowing which or how, that motivated an appeasement kind of worship. Rather than bringing a burden of guilt, as some would contend, Christianity brought freedom from guilt and a peace of mind never before known.

Soon we will have completed one full year in Nigeria. Life in a people-oriented culture has been more relaxing than in a goal-oriented one. As for me the "rat-race" is just that -- for the rats! But one thing really gets to me -- the weather. Henry belittles my weather-misery, but then he grew up in the Nashville Basin, not a lot different in the summer.

The humidity can be so smothering that I want to escape somewhere -- anywhere, just to get a deep breath! Whenever there is the slightest breeze, I stop whatever I'm doing to savor the moment. I hadn't realized how much I had said about it until I heard the kids playing Password one day. One of them drew the word "Breeze." The answer was a snap. He sighed deeply and did a perfect imitation of my saying, "Ooooh, feel that cooool ..."

Love,
Dit

Backdoor Medicine

Backdoor practice was illegal in Nigeria, but people had heard there was a doctor and they came. While Henry was volunteering his services at mission hospitals, I was left to deal with the sick at our backdoor. No one was more thankful to have nurses for relief than I.

Most came for headaches, malaria, diarrhea, or common first aid. Two frequent complaints took us longer to decipher -- "waist pain" and "internal heat." We finally decided that "waist pain" included sacroiliac strains from lifting and carrying such heavy loads on their heads. We had seen women stoop for a head load of bags so huge that it took two men to hoist up the load. Sometimes I thought they had malaria with its muscular pains and an enlarged liver and spleen. "Internal heat" we narrowed to anxiety.

At first I agreed to a kind of emergency backdoor clinic for the Bible students. Apparently eager for free medicine, they formed lines so long, I couldn't get my school teaching done. Being new I was hesitant to turn any away before determining how sick they really were. I was so grateful to Charla who came over one day to see how things were going. She saw the line, understood the situation, and said, "Go back to school. None of you is really sick."

I had heard that giving something with the left hand was like a curse. And I had heard left-handed missionaries tell how much difficulty they had remembering. But one day while holding something in my right, I gave a student medicine with my left, not thinking. He turned pale, trembled, and said, "I forgive you because you don't know our customs." If he hadn't been sick before, he was then.

Often our kind of medicine was the last resort after the native doctor had failed. Many cases were too far advanced for us to do anything. My heart really went out to them in their helpless situations. One lady holding a very anemic baby came saying he was her thirteenth and she had lost all the others. What could she do to keep from losing this one? I couldn't say, "Come back when we have a hospital." All I could do was suggest the nearest hospital, about 11 miles away.

One of the first to come to my door was a very poor, ragged couple holding a tiny bundle. They pulled back a piece of cloth to show me a weak, emaciated baby covered with a measles rash. Measles means death to most Nigerian children with no natural immunity. I asked Monday, "What do they want me to do?" He replied, "They want you to tell them whether the baby will live." Like the Biblical king who responded to Naaman, I was so astounded I answered, "Am I God!" Monday explained, "Madam, they have so little money. If you think the child can live, they will use it to take the child to the hospital. If you don't think it will live, they need their money to feed the others at home."

What should I say! There was no other missionary on campus at the moment for me to ask for advice. How could I say the child would live when he looked so ill and let them use their last penny? How could I say he would not if there was a faint possibility he might recover? I felt so overwhelmed I couldn't bring myself to answer. I retreated into the house to think and pray. When I returned the family had gone, but the haunting memory of them never shall.

Another couple seeking help for a tiny infant pulled back the wrapper to reveal a mass of blood in the diaper area. Completely puzzled I gave Monday a questioning glance. "Circumcision, Madam," he answered. "But this is a girl," I replied. His responding facial expression was one of wondering why I didn't know. Tropical diseases I had been briefed on, but this caught me completely off guard -- my first exposure to the genitalia mutilation known as female circumcision.

I began inquiring about the procedure -- what, why, and how. Some thought it was to keep their women chaste. Most had no explanation except, "It is our custom, Madam." As one said, "But, Madam, if we don't circumcise our female children, what are we supposed to do to them?"

The questioning necessary for a diagnosis taught me a lot about Nigerian life. One morning I was awakened at daybreak by hand clapping outside my door (Nigerian equivalent to our knocking). It was so early no one else was awake. Just as I reached the door, I met my steward coming to work. Interpreting he explained, "The lady was bitten by a dog, and the man is asking what they should do."

I replied, "Pen up the dog and observe it for two weeks to see if it is mad."

Monday replied, "They say they can't."

I answered, "Then tell them to kill the dog and save the head for testing."

Again he answered, "They say they can't," adding, "You see, they've already chopped (eaten) the head with the dog." I slapped my hand over my mouth and ran by the bedroom to wake up Henry for further details while I headed for the bathroom to lose the breakfast I hadn't yet eaten.

Nigerian Houseworkers

Emanuel Ekpendu
Our yardman

Tom Ibe
Our chef *extraordinaire*

Clement Ahiakwo & Monday John
Akpakpan, our stewards

John Ahukannah
Our washerman (1964)

Our Second Year
1965 - 1966

Missionary Kids. (standing in front): Becki Bryant: (1st row) Lee Farrar, David Bryant, Alicejoy Kee, David Farrar: (2nd row) Hank Farrar, Billy Rees Bryant, Sara Jo Bryant & Martha Farrar holding Debra Tarbet: (back row) Paul Kee & Paul Farrar holding Nancy Petty's foster child, Virginia (1967).

Outpatient Clinic
Nigerian Christian Hospital, Phase 1 (1965)

Dr. Farrar treats a child in the out-patient clinic. Note the white dry milk sack from USAID. (1965)

Dr. Farrar with malaria victim who has been painted by a native doctor. Nine people in this village were baptized that day.

Restored government rest house

First maternity patient with nurse assistant trainees. (1966)

The waiting room of the hospital's Out-Patient Clinic (1965)

Aug 11, 1965

Dear folks,

> "Water, water, everywhere
> And all the boards did shrink.
> Water, water everywhere,
> Nor any drop to drink."

Coleridge's Ancient Mariner had very little on us. Right now, according to Henry our biggest problem is, "Water! -- too much from above, and not enough from below." The rains have been so hard that the men have been unable to put down the pipe line from the stream to the clinic.

We purchased a water tank that has to be assembled but some essential parts and the instructions are missing. We might have been tempted to say WAWA (West Africa Wins Again), but this was an European error!

Anthony Agali and his crew have constructed a 30 foot monument to Nigerian ingenuity and craftsmanship. First Anthony designed the mold for steel reinforced concrete pillars, then homemade ladders. Headpan by headpan style, using both hand and both feet to scale the ladders the workers balanced the concrete mix on their heads until a man at the top lifted the pan and poured it into the molds.

Now John Morgan, "worth his weight in gold" as Henry says, is up on top of the columns every day instructing the men how to assemble the tank. He seems to be really enjoying it and Henry refers to it as "John's erector set." In this land of "specialization" the Nigerians are astonished that one man knows how to do so many things -- doctor, preacher, and now engineer.

The pump house has been completed and the generator is being installed today. Saturday the Senior Medical Officer from Aba came to inspect the clinic and gave his approval to open whenever Henry felt it was ready. The nurses have been busy with their tests and interviews to select ten young local women to train as nurse assistants.

Two weeks ago Henry brought home a baby genet that someone had found in the top of a palm when they cut it down. Its eyes were not yet open. Marty was thrilled to take over its care, feeding it with a medicine dropper and poking tiny bits of ground beef into its mouth. She takes it to her room at night and is up for its 6 a.m.

feeding. Now it sucks eagerly on the dropper and takes the beef from our hands. She's even been giving it vitamin drops and antimalarials. It weighed in at 6 ounces on arrival, and the kids are so happy it has gained two.

We had no idea what it was until we looked in our book of West African mammals. According to that book it was probably the first domesticated cat, the holy cat tamed by the Egyptians. The face is like our cats with a longer nose and lower set eyes. Its body shape reminds me more of a weasel. The coloring is somewhat like a tabby with lovely black and gray markings. The most unusual feature is the long ringed tail, as long as its body. It is gentle like a kitten and purrs like one, but agile like a wild animal. Just watching him lope about has given us all hours of amusement. Lee goes around with him draped over his shoulder most of the day. They've named him "Tigger" after the bouncy character in the Winnie-the-Pooh stories.

Ever since we came Lee and Hank have admired the way our water carriers can walk uphill for about 500 feet and up the concrete steps to our barrels with a four gallon tin of water on their heads and never touch it with their hands or lose a drop until they empty it into the barrels. One day Hank and Lee took small plastic buckets and headed for the stream to test their skills. By the time they reached the house most of their water had thoroughly soaked them. Hank reached up to remove an almost empty bucket with, "I tell you, this water carrying isn't as much fun as it looks."

The older children have put away their schoolbooks for a two week vacation, but Donna wants to work with the younger ones as long as she is here. The campus is so quiet now with the Bible students on "holiday." They've gone out two by two on evangelistic campaigns. Our Bible College congregation provides their transportation to go, and the church where they work will give them food, lodging, and return transportation. Two who speak Hausa have gone to the North to work with Moses Opara, our Nigerian missionary there. With Monday out of school, we're tackling the housecleaning and waxing floors and furniture again before another term begins.

Just as Donna was beginning to wonder if she'd ever see the sun before she left, the sky has turned a bright blue. It's called the "August break," a short dry period usually the first two weeks of August when all will be hot and sticky again.

We (Henry, the nurses, and I) have just returned from speaking at the Efik women's annual lectureship which is scheduled during school break at Ukpom Bible College. About 400 women had trekked and cycled for miles with their cooking pots, sleeping mats, and nursing babies. Henry was given the subject of family worship, the nurses assigned hygiene, but mine was tops, "Refuting Superstitions about Childbirth." First I had to read and talk to women just to see what they believed. As Donna put it, "It's hard to believe we are all living in the same generation."

Henry drew me some lovely illustrations for my lectures on just how babies are formed and what happens at birth. Twins in the past were commonly killed and the mother driven out because it was said she had been with the devil who had fathered one. Now such practices are illegal, but those who know say most husbands still put away a wife who has had twins privately because she is "spoiled." Even doctors in local hospitals say that the mother of twins along with the babies often dies mysteriously in the hospital. They believe they were poisoned.

It is a common belief that the spirit of a deceased ancestor will try to take the baby away if they fail to name it after the right one so they must go to a doctor of spirits ("witch doctor") with money and sacrifices so he can tell them for whom it should be named.

Some come from areas that still have fattening room for brides and make them gorge to become more productive. I also tried to explain how female circumcision could cause lifelong problems sometimes damaging the urethra or cause hard scars and infections that could complicate childbirth later. These are just a few of their superstitions that I covered.

Good help here means finding a person who understands English and is so basically honest he will do whatever you say even when it makes no sense to him. Charla and Friday Onukafor trained Mark Apollos who became the cook-steward for the nurses. Doug taught Friday, who was their cook, to drive so he became "our man Friday" running all those daily errands to Aba for the whole compound. With both Lawyer's cook and steward in other jobs that would leave no one to help the next family. Charla, Monday, and I worked with a young man eager to learn, but we told Donna when she arrived that he wasn't really trained yet.

One evening Donna invited the nurses to dinner and felt comfortable enough with his cooking ability to give him a lemon ice box pie recipe with a crumb crust for their dessert explaining, "You do not bake the crust for this one."

When dessert was served, they put in their forks to discover something was amiss. True to instructions, he had not baked the crust. Instead he had neatly fitted the crumb crust inside of a raw pastry one. As soon as he left the room they laughed hilariously, but quickly smothered the laughter when he returned.

We are planning a surprise farewell party for the Morgans next Monday. Patti Bryant is sewing Nigerian garments to give them. John has been able to see diseases and practice medicine in a way not possible a Vanderbilt, and the water tank will be a lasting memorial. Donna can laugh at the way she screamed the first time a lizard popped out at her when she opened the oven door to light it, and the kids will miss their teacher. They've been so much fun and so much help. It's been a better summer for all of us because they came.

Love,
Dit

August 24, 1965

Dear folks,

The Morgans are up late tonight packing to leave at the crack of dawn. So I'm also up late writing this for them to mail in the U.S. Everyday has been so full. I intend to write, but my days go too fast. Henry is stretched out on the couch, exhausted from a day of surgery at the Itu leprosarium. Paul, working on a first class Scout badge, has just returned from practicing the Morse Code with Dr. Morgan. As I write Marty and the younger boys are in bed. Earlier she and Sara Jo Bryant presented one of their puppet shows as a farewell for the Morgans. The Dunn's three small children from Ukpom were fascinated with the puppets.

We can't tell you how much we hate to see the Morgans go, and they seem to hate to leave. Besides her marvelous, cheerful personality, Donna has been such a help as a teacher, a secretary, and a worker in the clinic. John, a mechanic as well as a doctor, has supervised the installation of the water tank, the pump, and the generator. Some parts ordered for the pump have not yet arrived, so even tonight he is explaining to Henry where they are to go. I don't know how the clinic could have begun without his expertise.

The biggest news is the opening of the clinic. Saturday we had a big formal opening with all the chiefs and the councilmen present. We were to have had a ribbon-cutting at the clinic, but typical of our Nigerian weather, the torrential rains made it necessary for us to meet in the school building instead. Henry made an excellent dedicatory address and quoted Scripture in both Ibo and Efik, much to the audience's delight. Every part of the program had to be interpreted into three languages -- Ibo, Efik, and English -- which took three times as long.

The head of the Eastern Ngwa County Council, who had opposed the clinic strongly in the beginning, was not only present, but even presented Henry with his personal check for approximately $60, possibly moved more by politics than mercy when he looked out over about 500 people crammed into the little building and reconsidered his original position. After the program everyone was served refreshments according to the Nigerians' custom -- rice with beef fried in palm oil and hot peppers, ground nuts (peanuts), Pepsis, and Kola nuts.

On Monday, August 23, we began seeing patients, and, as you might expect, were flooded. Registration was halted around 2 p.m. after about 200, and even then there was time to see only about half of those. The others were given numbers and told to return Wednesday. Many had even brought bottles to the formal opening hoping to receive medicine then. These were not hypochondriacs, but very ill people who had never had a doctor available before.

The nurses, Nancy and Iris, have tested and interviewed about 400 prospects to select six most qualified to train as nurse assistants. With no time to begin training before the clinic opened, they have been pleased at how quickly the girls learn. To fulfill a request of the land donors we are having classes for their sons and daughters with Henry, Nancy and me as tutors.

During our August break the past two weeks, I've been cleaning drawers, shelves, etc. and painting. Now I am ready and eager to devote my time to school teaching all five this year -- that's grades 1, 2, 5, 6, and 8.

Earlier this evening we had a send-off devotional at our house for the Morgans with families from Ukpom and Ikot Usen and our workers. The church that meets on campus presented Dr. Morgan with a white Nigerian costume. We plan to be up at 5 a.m. to see them off at Port Harcourt, and it is now 11:15 p.m. Good night.

Love,
Dit

September 10, 1965

Dear folks,

    A doctor will always be the last to admit he really should be a patient. When Henry was hit with exhaustion, low-grade fever, and irritability, he said, "Tension, worry, and anxiety ---- trying to get the clinic opened before John had to go." When he lost his appetite and had waves of nausea, he said, "Stress." But when he turned "as yellow as a punkin,'" he had run out of answers. A trip to Delta Clinic, Port Harcourt, confirmed what he'd really suspected all along -- hepatitis. He thinks he picked it up from surgery at one of the mission hospitals, but he gave us all gamma globulin shots anyway.

    The clinic is open three days a week -- 7 to 12 a.m. and 2 to 5 p.m. on Mondays, Wednesdays, and Fridays. He got in one clinic day before he was obviously jaundiced, and now bedrest for a month is the best treatment. The nurses are managing the clinic -- off to a good start with over 100 a day registering. At home I have to keep the curtains pulled. The Nigerians looking in the house wouldn't understand why their doctor can walk around inside the house but not be at the clinic helping them.

    When the nurses told the people that if they felt very ill they should go to a hospital, some said, "No. We'll wait till he comes back. We haven't felt so well in years as we have since he first saw us."

    Doug and Rees had been negotiating for months with the local chiefs and land owners, and it is now official - 119.4 acres joining the Bible School property will be signed over for the establishment of a hospital and houses for personnel. This does not mean that they can afford to pay for the construction. Even the money to convert the old rest house into a clinic came from America. In exchange we have agreed to train their children and give them first choice of available jobs. They will continue to farm the land until it is needed for hospital use.

We expect the missing part to the pump to arrive from England in three months. In the meantime the Lord has provided enough water from above to keep the clinic going.

Barely into the school year we are already meeting new challenges. One of Paul's subjects is poetry appreciation. Since Paul ia a very fact-oriented person, he sees little value in poetry. Henry has a great appreciation for all the arts, and with him at home I've turned that subject over to him. He'll undoubtedly do a better job than I.

Since Hank has learned to read well, he and Lee both enjoy Hank's reading aloud the stories from his books. When I brought out Dick and Jane for Lee, he was quick to inform me, "I'm not going to read that dumb stuff! I want real stories." What next! I can't help but appreciate his discernment, and after all, that's the beauty of home schooling -- tailoring the curriculum to the child.

Paul is the only one who has not had a friend his age on campus. The American families at Aba Textile Mills with children Paul's age have sent them back to the USA for schooling except one with a 14 year old son. Paul is spending today (Friday) with him in Aba, then he will spend time here with Paul until his parents come for church Sunday. When I heard the Underwoods would be coming with a 13-year-old daughter, I was so excited I said, "Finally, Paul, there will someone your own age!" He stuck his head down and muttered, "I don't know why it couldn't have been a boy." I couldn't resist, "You might be surprised how interesting she can become in another year."

Love,
Dit

September 26, 1965

Dear folks,

Only time heals hepatitis. Henry's drive exceeds his energy level, but he did work three half-days at the clinic this past week before having to spend the afternoons resting. He still has some jaundice.

Our big news here has been the arrival of David and Myra Underwood and their three -- Becky (age 13), David (almost 10), and "Brian Bris" (eight months). David will replace Doug Lawyer as principal of the Bible Training College. A new family always boosts morale and brings a flurry of welcoming parties from both the missionaries and the local Christians. Marty and Sara Jo Bryant were so happy to have another girl they gave Becky a welcoming their style -- a pajama party last night.

Yesterday Myra accompanied me to a Christian ladies' fellowship where I spoke on "Train Up a Child in the Way He Should Go." When I was preparing my first talk for the Nigerian women, the best advice came from Mary Lou Curry, "Never speak down to them." Remembering those word each time, I prepare as carefully as I would for American ladies. English is the official language and school books are in English. There will always be some who need no interpreter, especially younger women. For those who need interpretation I can't help but wonder what is being done to my carefully prepared lessons.

The women of the local congregations commonly have dawn devotionals before going to work in the farms, but these monthly area-wide fellowships are special highlights. They come dressed in their best to study, sing, visit, and prepare a meal together. Frequently they invite one of the missionary women to speak.

Sharing Myra's first time to travel bush roads, see local markets in action, and worship in a mud building brought back the excitement of my first experiences. She saw so much to appreciate that I had allowed to become commonplace such as the roadside profusion of ferns and caladium, the bright-eyed children streaming out of compounds to yell "Becca" as we passed, the colorful clothing, and the enthusiastic singing. I'm eager to see her reaction to the Sunday afternoon class of about a hundred children sitting with rapt attention for only one teacher. It couldn't be done in America.

The campus menagerie is growing. And so is our genet. One of the kids is always carrying him around, and he responds with affectionate purrs. Now in addition to their rabbits and puppy, the Bryants have a baby civet. It is larger than our genet, is not as playful, and has a musk gland. Also the nurses have acquired two cats from a British lady who was leaving Nigeria and wanted to be sure her pets didn't become, shall I say, "cat food."

David created an ant farm (Henry says the last thing we need to grow more of around here) and keeps a praying mantis for which he catches grasshoppers. The other day he found an ant lion and dropped it into his ant farm. Whether it was another of his entomology experiments or just to liven things up a bit I wouldn't know, but probably both.

Yesterday our Scout troop sponsored a bicycle rodeo on the tennis court including safety checks on the bikes, a written test they developed, and a skills test they devised. We ended with a picnic and everyone had fun. Their all day cycling trip with Iris and this rodeo completes their cycling badges.

I think Scouting gives the girls a well-planned program for personal development and service as well as a connection with girls around the world. Patti Bryant volunteered to teach then sewing, so Marty is making her first dress -- quite an accomplishment for an eleven-year-old. Another project that has sparked their enthusiasm and also been a valuable contribution to the mission has been helping Patti with the puppet theater for children's Bible classes. The Nigerian children have never seen anything like it before, but it would be hard to say who enjoys it the most -- those watching or those performing.

Love,
Dit

October 18, 1965

Dear folks,

Today, for the first time in three months, Henry was able to meet a preaching appointment. He's more rested because we've just returned from a short vacation in Enugu. There's really no way he can get the rest he needs to recover here. The workers and I have been kept busy turning people away because they see him out occasionally and don't understand why he needs to rest. We still keep the curtains and doors closed so people can't see him move about inside the house, or they will yell at him demanding attention.

Last week we had word that the C. L. Pattersons of Houston had deposited $100 into our personal account. Money comes in almost daily for the medical work, but this is the first time anyone has given for our personal use. Since we needed to go to Enugu anyway to see if we could get the hospital plans approved, we decided to use the money for a vacation. When Iris heard about the gift, she squealed with delight and said, "This is the answer to our prayers. Nancy and I have been wondering how we could get him away long enough to really rest." Our visits to the zoo, the swimming pool, the pottery, and toyland in the air-conditioned Kingsway department store with "I'm Dreaming of a White Christmas" playing, and our time with the Curry and Keesee families was relaxing for us all.

Finally we do have the approval of the Minister of Health for the hospital plans we submitted. After working for months carefully designing what he considered an ideal plan, Henry scrapped it all. Every time he submitted his own plans, the officials found something else they wanted revised. Finally he said, "Forget it! We'll just submit their own preapproved plans. We can update after we get their approval." Guess what! They even found things they wanted changed with those too. But now all that is behind us. Green Lawn Church of Christ, Lubbock, Texas, has told us they are willing to take the oversight in collecting funds for the construction.

I just hope Henry feels up to a crucial day tomorrow. Chiefs and elders from three villages along with the trustees for the church in Nigeria will meet with a Divisional Officer to sign over 119.4 acres of choice land on the Aba-Ikot Ekpene Road for building a hospital. We currently operate the out-patient clinic on land owned by the government. The hospital acreage adjoins that and the land given for the Bible School.

The missionaries, especially Rees and Doug, have worked hard for the past year to get a verbal agreement. Today all the local officials have been coming and going in order to go over the deed carefully and ask any questions that they may have before they sign tomorrow. All of which keeps me coming and going all day with the tea cups. As I write it is 10:30 p.m. Henry and Rees are still out in one of the villages going over some points in the deed that were troubling to one chief.

An amusing thing, if it can be called that, is a rivalry between two of the chiefs. Neither is a Christian and they are so jealous of one another they wouldn't come to a previous meeting at the same time. Even for our formal opening of the clinic they came at different times. To sign the deed they will both have to be present in the same room at the same time. We are wondering if, in giving land for a Christian cause, we might say Christianity brought them together in a way nothing else could.

Levi Kennedy, Mr. and Mrs. F.F. Carson, and another lady from Calif. arrived in Nigeria Thursday for a three weeks visit. They have been at Ukpom, but will be with us tomorrow. Brother Kennedy from near Chicago has been preaching since 1921 and now preaches for the largest black congregation in the States.

Brother Carson preaches for a church in Richmond, Calif. Both visited Nigeria about two years ago and since then have enthusiastically supported works here morally and financially. Brother Carson gave Henry a check for $675, a one night contribution from his church, after he had spoken about the needs of the hospital.

Brother Kennedy has had some edema in his feet that he has conferred about with Henry. He said some in his congregation felt he should not make the trip because of his health, but he told them he'd be just as close to heaven from Nigeria as he would from Chicago.

Patti Bryant says it's unbelievable to her how many visitors we have, especially when she stops to recall a time when their family were the only expatriates she knew about in the area.

Love,
Dit

November 16, 1965

Dear folks,

Our family has reached a new milestone -- our first teenager has "arrived." To celebrate Paul's thirteenth birthday, Nov. 4, we took all the children to the Aba television station where the manager, the friend who trained at RCA, New York, took them on a tour then let them watch themselves on TV. Afterward we went to the Aba Club for a swimming party.

Halloween was two days of fun. Saturday night they went to a costume party at Ukpom. With no "5 & 10" their costumes were masterful creations of originality. Marty was a gorgeous Cinderella in a blue formal with jewelry and make-up, her blonde hair piled high under a tiara. But it was so hot the costumes came off half an hour after they got there.

Sunday night they dressed up again to go trick or treat on our campus. By now the workers know our holiday customs and enjoy them too. Later the kids met at our house for a spook house the older ones had devised. They were having so much fun I had to go through it myself. They had even made jack-o-lanterns out of a native green squash (about the size of a large grapefruit).

Today Henry felt up to making his first trip to Queen Elizabeth Hospital to perform surgery since July. He has been seeing about 150 patients a day for three days a week at our clinic. Every one is a pathetic story. To relate one, a fifteen year old girl had delivered in the bush -- no prenatal care, the baby had died, and her family brought her five miles on the back of a bicycle convulsing all the way.

Nancy and Iris have divided the nursing responsibilities so that Nancy will serve as the matron, a British term for the nursing care supervisor, and Iris will be the director of nursing education.

Iris has been developing an American style nursing program for her nurse assistant trainees, though without a hospital we cannot have an officially registered school. Iris and Nancy will know what their students have been taught rather than trying to undo another's teaching. There is such a critical shortage in health care that the government operates village dispensaries with workers who have had only a few weeks basic training in the most frequently encountered illnesses such as malaria, worms, diarrheas, etc. Also private physicians usually have a private clinic where they train their own workers. Some of these have already applied to us as "trained nurses."

Nancy patrols the clinic. She has tried hard to impress on the registration clerks that everyone must receive a number in the order in which they came and will be seen in that order except for emergencies. Contrary to local custom, there will be no "big" (important) men pushing the "little people" aside to be seen first. The test came when a large military man appeared and insisted on being seen immediately. The registrar gave him a number and said, "To be seen sooner, you must get permission from Sister (British term for nurse in charge)."

The man found Nancy and announced, " I am (rank and name) and I have come from the Congo (of the Nigerian peacekeeping force). I want to see the doctor."

Nancy straightened herself to her full five-foot-three and answered, "And I am Nancy Petty. I came from Bear Creek, Tennessee. And you, sir, will have to wait in line like everyone else."

To remodel the old government rest house into a clinic, the Ministry of Health insisted that we had to have indoor toilets. Such is not the village custom. But Nancy was determined that if we had to go to the trouble and expense of installing them, the people were going to use them. Violators found themselves startled into learning that it is possible to stop mid-stream.

A major request of the landowners in deeding the land for the hospital was jobs for their children. The missionaries agreed to train their children with the possibility of employment later if they proved capable. For those who asked, "What if I have no children?" we said, "You can select someone." We should have realized that appointments to the class would go to the highest bidder. As with so many oppressed people, bribery and cheating are viewed more often as ways to get ahead rather than being intrinsically wrong.

Henry, Nancy, and I teach the classes for this group. My subjects are hygiene, anatomy, and physiology. When I gave the exam, one of my better students asked me how I could grade it since everyone cheated including herself. Actually it wasn't difficult. Out of approximately one hundred papers, five had passing grades. My test question were designed to see if they could use the information I taught in actual medical situations and not rote memory, which is the mainstay for Nigerian schools.

Next month Monday will be completing the Bible School, valedictorian out of eleven graduates, and leaving us. With no free schools in Nigeria, older siblings are expected to help the younger with school fees at least to standard six, our equivalent to grade eight. On the $12/mo. from us, Monday manages to pay his own expenses and help with the younger children.

Government secondary schools have a maximum entrance age limit of 18, and Monday says he knows he is 22. When asked how he knows, he says, "My mother wrote it our Bible" -- unusual here. The Otoyos, administrators of the Christian secondary school at Ukpom, are allowing him to enter there because most students wouldn't know their age anyway. He has shown the kind of intelligence, dedication, and Christian character that makes us want to help him financially, a worthy investment in the future of the church in Nigeria. Henry has also taught Monday to drive, which will be an asset to his future since most Nigerians cannot.

I asked Monday to select another preaching student to train as a steward before he goes. He has chosen Clement Ahiakwo who seems pleasant and capable, but for our family, especially our kids, there will never be another Monday.

Nigerian schools are year round except for breaks in spring, August and winter. The winter breaks are longest going from December to mid-January. It's more convenient here for us to have our home school breaks at the same time rather than follow an American schedule.

With so many Texans and Tennesseans here, I was happy to know another Hoosier was on his way to Ukpom. I was even more surprised to learn he came from the little town of Huron where his family knew my mother's family -- even the same country ridge -- Mike King from King's Ridge. Our other Hoosiers, Philip Dunn and family, will be leaving soon because of health problems.

Rees encourages churches to have a policy to disfellowship polygamists. Last Sunday he was supporting a preacher's efforts, when one of the polygamists in the church spoke up and asked, "But who would support my wives?" Rees suggested sending them back to their families. The next question was, "But I own much land. Who would farm it?" Rees answered, "Which are you worried about -- supporting your wives or your wives supporting you?" To exemplify the dedication of many, one second year Bible student could have had all five years of his secondary school free because his father gave land to the Catholic church, but he has chosen instead to study the Bible with us.

As it's getting cooler by the day there, it gets hotter by the day here. Henry says, "Look on the bright side. Think of all those in America paying for a sauna, and you have a natural one."

Love,
Dit

November 30, 1965

Dear folks,

Bible School (BTC) graduation here is a big event for everyone. Last night we had a faculty-student dinner with the faculty providing huge pots of rice with chunks of meat fried in palm oil and lots of hot pepper, the way the Nigerians like it. Meat is scarce, so it was a treat for us to watch the students enjoy it so much. Monday said he didn't know how fat people managed because he ate so much he could hardly make it up the hill afterward.

Today has been track and field day. These young preachers are excellent athletes despite their lack of training. The kids cheered as

Monday placed second in the 100-yard dash. Tomorrow will be lectureship day. I'm eager to hear Moses Opara again, our Ibo missionary to the Muslim north. Even though his life is in danger, he now has a congregation of about 25 Christians, including Muslim converts, at Gusau. Thursday will be graduation day.

Friday will be a day of fellowship before the holiday break. The men will have a conference in the morning, and in the afternoon we plan a farewell for the Dunn family and the Youngs, Floyd and Marie. Floyd has been in charge of constructing the Shell Oil Refinery at Port Harcourt, now completed, and they have worshipped with us regularly, helping us in many, many ways.

Our oil company friends of Port Harcourt supplied a turkey and all the trimmings for a Thanksgiving feast for all at our house. Sunday we had a big ice cream supper with the Youngs and two other Port Harcourt couples who worship with us. Last night I had a coconut curry dinner honoring a Peace Corps girl who has been working in Aba but will be returning home to Los Angeles. I had thought when I planned to go to Nigeria that I was going to the dropping-off place, but I have never done so much entertaining in my life.

On Nov. 20, we were guests of Judge A. E. Bassey, agent-general of Eastern Nigeria, for the formal opening of his hat factory in Ikot Ekpene. The Premier of the Eastern Region was the featured speaker, and they fired a nine-gun salute at his arrival. Afterward we were given a tour of the plant which plans to make raffia hats of all styles for both local and foreign markets, hopefully competing with panama hats. This was followed by a hat style show, refreshments, and entertainment including masked dancers on stilts. The day concluded with a big dinner for the invited guests.

Last Saturday we attended the diamond (75th) anniversary of the Mary Slessor Hospital, Itu, one of the mission hospitals where Henry has been working. From there we visited Calabar. The Cross River near the Delta is so much wider than our Mississippi that we spent an hour and a half on the ferry crossing to Calabar. We saw many historically interesting places including the grave of Mary Slessor. In America I had never heard of her, but every student of Nigerian history knows how this brave young single Scottish lady of the 19th century snatched twins from those who would have killed them to raise them herself, introduced Christianity to the most pagan tribes feared by others, and became their beloved "White Ma."

Old Calabar was once the chief port of the Bight of Biafra where missionaries and gin came in, and slaves and palm oil went out. Today Itu and Calabar are very different from the more industrialized cities of Aba and Port Harcourt we are familiar with. There are large colonial mansions built on high ground for the British officials, and below them are row on row of mud houses built so close that viewed from the hills they look like a sea of brown thatch.

The Harmattan has arrived. Iris says, "It's still not as bad as a Texas dust storm." It also brings the graceful egrets and right now from my window I can count twenty.

The genet has been a joy to us all. Henry said that when he was on bedrest and everyone was busy with school, his chief amusement was watching Tigger's antics and agility. Marty monitors his nutrition and growth. At present his body is ten inches long and his ringed tail is ten inches long.

The Bryants have not been as successful with their civet. It died though Patti tried her best to save it -- even bought goat's milk which had helped her own babies.

An animal pet is not part of the Nigerian culture. Their dogs may be guards, a main course, or the sewage disposal system especially if the compound has a bare bottomed toddler -- but not a companion. They bring us small animals for pets hoping for a few shillings.

Once they brought me a potto, another animal I had to look up in my book. It reminded me so much of an opossum -- light hair, beady eyes behind a pointed nose, and razor sharp teeth that snapped at everything in sight. Not knowing what else to do with it, I dropped it in the old rabbit cage for the night. The next morning the door had been opened and he was gone. I had also read that he was nocturnal and had prehensile stubby second toes and fingers. Perhaps he opened the door himself. Perhaps a night watchman had a good meal the next day. Whatever happened, he was so vicious I couldn't feel it was a big loss.

Our kids can't believe how unfeeling the native children are to small animals like toads and lizards. One day a boy brought me a beautiful iridescent blue bird for sale, but I didn't want to take in birds. He broke the bird's wing so it would not escape while he played with it. No one has ever taught them that animals are gifts from God for us to protect and care for.

Dean Beckloff was ten last week and David will be soon. To celebrate we had a real wiener roast outdoors with birthday cake, ice cream, and strawberries. We found hot dogs in Port Harcourt for $1.65/lb and strawberries the same price for one pint. It was a big splurge, but a true celebration since the children hadn't tasted either for a year. We make birthdays and holidays very special occasions here.

Love,
Dit

January 1, 1966

Dear folks,

Our little foil Christmas tree and its miniature electric lights are back in the shoe box. The children's Christmas art work is gone from the walls and windows. Paul has declared, "This house looks naked."

With the Bryants and nurses vacationing in Enugu, we and the Underwoods took our families to Port Harcourt last evening to see "Savage Sam", sequel to "Old Yeller." Returning home just before midnight, we saw churches all along the way holding all night services. Without electricity they were lighted by bush lanterns (kerosene) or Tilley lamps. Bonfires glowed outside. Usually all would have been quiet at that hour, but last night those not in churches were parading along the roads singing and dancing, shooting firecrackers, or piling palm frond and debris in the road like Halloween pranksters. We had to watch carefully all the way home. When we arrived home at 11:55, the kids made a mad dash for the firecrackers they'd bought in the market earlier.

Usually the missionary families from all three stations -- Onicha Ngwa, Ukpom, and Ikot Usen -- have a Christmas feast together rotating locations. Last year they met on our campus. Although Henry is now working full time, he tires more easily than before hepatitis, so we opted for a quieter day. To escape the heat we drove to Azumini in the afternoon, where the Imo River runs crystal clear. Standing on the bridge it seemed you could count every sand grain through twenty feet of water. The kids took stale bread to feed the fish and ducks. The most fun was throwing pennies into the water to watch the little naked boys dive down and retrieve them. There is also a fish hatchery and a beach.

A strong Harmattan blew in today bringing temperatures down into the 60's. This much wind is so seldom, the kids are out trying to fly a kite. Henry has asthma and Lee has an ear infection because the dust gives him nasal congestion.

In his valedictory speech Monday said: "Every building has an architect, every painting has a painter, every newspaper its printer, and every design a designer. Think of me as a building, the Nicks were my architect; as a painting the Masseys were the painters; as a paper the Farrars has been the printers; and these (pointing to the faculty) have been my designers." His speech was one of so much gratitude, optimism, and faith, I told him I wanted a copy so I could read it whenever I wondered what I was doing here. Nancy said, "When Monday goes a lot of sunshine will leave this campus."

I found a book on handicrafts for Nigerian schools with a lot of useful ideas for my own. Ant hill clay soaked in water until malleable makes an excellent modeling clay and can be baked and painted. The termites ("white ants") bring their dirt up from under the top sandy soil and mix it with saliva so it can harden like concrete. I might add that salt and flour clay such as we use in America doesn't work. There is so much moisture in the air that it continues taking up water until it runs. I found someone who could show our children how to make baskets, and raffia is for sale. Marty keeps a "scrap box" under her bed for cardboard rolls, bits of yarn and fabric, small boxes, colored paper, etc. and surprises us with very creative puppets, cards, and gifts.

Wishing you the best year ever,

Love,
Dit

We depended on Henry's brother George and his wife Evelyn to look after our business in America. They also sent us things we could not locate in Nigeria.

January 16, 1966

Dear George, Evelyn, and girls,

Thank you for doing our shopping and for so many things you do for us. We couldn't continue here without help from that side.

I can picture our families listening to the radio and searching the papers for the latest news on the attempted military coup yesterday. Before you receive this, you will know the outcome. Let me assure you that we in the Eastern Region are a long way from Lagos -- several hundred miles.

In an election several weeks ago two major parties were vying for power -- one representing the Muslim North and the other a combination of elements mostly from the West and Midwest. The Northerners, who control the government, were said to have jammed the ballot boxes and riots have ensued since. It all came to a head yesterday when part of the army rebelled. The premier of the North and some of his ministers were killed, and they kidnapped the prime minister.

Nigeria is like three separate countries in languages, religion, culture, and types of local government. The turmoil has been in the West and North where the tribes intermingle. The East, where we live, has been more politically united behind another party, and we are not expecting such problems here.

The Houston Ezells and John Dedmans of Nashville are constructing buildings at Ukpom in a mass production style that leaves the Nigerians amazed. During their three weeks here, they have put up five buildings -- two dorms and three tutor's homes ready to roof. Houston shared his trade secret. When workers began putting up their tools an hour before quitting time he surprised them with, "We're not through yet!"

Efforts to renew their visas locally were denied, so they made a trip to Lagos by car ready to return to America if necessary, but they had no problems with extensions. They returned through the West just in time for the coup. We were so happy to see them safely back because there are always hoodlums ready to take advantage of any unrest. They reported that they did meet road blocks, but were just waved through. Now they can stay till Feb 10., and we hope help a little with the hospital.

We enjoyed a brief visit from Brother Gene Peden last week. There's no good way for visitors to notify us when they will be coming and no other place for them to stay with safe water and safe food handling other than with missionaries when they do. With no corner grocery, I stay prepared for the unexpected.

It's impossible for these quick visits and survey trips to give a true picture of our work, problems, or daily life. Mary Lou said on their first tour, when they were taking turns entertaining a short term visitor, each family prepared the best they had for the guest. When he concluded, "You people certainly do eat well," she decided it was time for reality. Thank you for seeing about so many things for us. We are all well except for Lee's chronic ear infections.

Love,
Grace

February 13, 1966

Dear folks,

Your letters about snow really make me homesick. Here we are in the midst of the "slash and burn" season. Every day the air is filled with smoke as fires crackle close around us. When the fires begin, the hawks circle overhead ready to feast on the lizards and small rodents trying to escape. Sometimes I wonder if they are trying to smoke us out too.

In America we would never think of starting fires when the vegetation is so dry. It's been a marvel to me how they can contain the fires. Fronds on the palms burn, new ones come out, and the tree lives on. Planting is a hands-on job done mostly by the women stooping over short handled hoes. They scrape the weeds into piles around the roots of bushes. Recalling all the new ground I had helped clear as a child, I asked one of the workers, "Why don't you just dig out the roots of the bushes instead of always working around them? Then you will have more land for planting." He answered, "But, Madam, what would we do for sticks?"

It hadn't occurred to me before what vital uses sticks have in the local culture -- cooking fuel, building material, and fencing, to name a few. Interestingly, sticks stuck closely in the ground for a fence will often sprout leaves becoming a living fence.

They have a general principle that the land should lie fallow for three or four years between cultivation. But sometimes the need for food shortens that time. Cassava stems are cut into short lengths for planting and produce a root they harvest. Yams are grown from the eye of a seed yam like our potato. In addition to these two staples they grow chiefly okra, maize (our corn), hot peppers, large fluted pumpkins for the seeds and leaves, and a small round green squash.

Garden plots are very small, not separated by fences as we might. I ask, "How do you know where your 'piece' ends and another's begins?" The only answer I've received has been, "We know." I see ridges that I presume to be dividing lines, but with this sandy loam constantly shifting they can't be permanent. A surveyor put up concrete markers for the hospital land, but there are differences of opinion on the boundaries of the BTC property.

I wonder what, if anything, is being reported in America about the Nigerian coup. Our news comes via Voice of America (VOA) in special broadcasts to Africa, so we hear a lot. The coup has had no noticeable effect on our lives. The local people I've talked to consider it a good thing. Some of the high officials who have been skimming revenues off the top have preferred suicide to surrendering to the army. The man in charge of Peace Corps activities in our region is a black Christian. When he and his wife came to worship with us Sunday. he said the American government was not concerned about their welfare.

The Ezells and Dedmans ended their two months tour last week. In the three days they spent on hospital construction, they accomplished an astonishing amount. After sewing 100 school uniforms at Ukpom, the women made something personal for each missionary. They asked what we needed most, then did pajamas for Henry and a dress for me.

Our maternity ward is almost completed, and two more buildings, men's ward and kitchen/laundry, are going up. The most urgent medical need appears to be maternity care so that ward will be our first building to open. Barney Morehead sent about $7000 for the hospital. The money came from a Bro. Kent Smith of Ohio who willed it to him to be used for missionary work however he wished.

We plan to close the clinic and go to the Obudu Ranch, where we vacationed last year, for the week of Feb. 28 - Mar 5 along with the nurses. Obudu is on the edge of the Western Cameroonian mountain range, a mile high, so I've been digging the long sleeved shirts and sweaters out of the storage barrel, where they've spent the past year. We won't see snow, but it will at least be a relief from this heat. February is probably the most miserable month of the year here.

Love,
Dit

March 15, 1966

Dear folks,

I have concluded that we do not have "African vacations." We have "African adventures." If we do get some badly needed rest, we are soon worn out by the long, hot journey home so that we need another vacation to recuperate from the first.

We had such a great time at Obudu last year, we were eager for another. This year was entirely different. Only our family, the nurses, and a Peace Corps couple on honeymoon were there, but one by one all, except me, came down with chills and high fever followed by diarrhea. Henry suspected Salmonella because the toxic symptoms preceded the intestinal ones and because I was unaffected. As a child I was seriously ill with typhoid, so I apparently had more immunity than is given by typhoid shots.

The Obudu guest house is one of the most highly recommended in Nigeria, but we recognize that it's always an eat-out-at-your-own-risk proposition anywhere here. We travel with medicines for any eventuality. By the week-end we were able to make the trip home, but the nurses are still suffering in spite of treatment.

It's disheartening to wait a year for a vacation then have to pay their standard $30/day for food we couldn't eat because of an illness they gave us. We were even charged extra for cokes when we couldn't tolerate their solid food. The managers have a standard plan set by the government and they won't allow for any exceptions. Had this happened in America the place would have been closed until the cause of the infection was solved. But this is not America, and we must plan accordingly.

Poor Henry! He's always telling me to look on the bright side when this miserable climate gets to me. One day when he was unable to make it to the table because of dizziness and cramping, I couldn't resist, "Just look on the bright side. You said all you wanted was a change in climate and some rest." (You'll be happy to know recent liver function tests show no liver damage from his hepatitis.)

Now, back in our "Turkish bath," daily temperatures soar over 90 and the high humidity adds another fifteen degrees to the heat index. Many nights I can't sleep till I move onto the cool concrete floor without even a sheet. I was surprised to hear Myra confess she did the same.

Local people have had high hopes that the new military government would improve their lot economically by cleaning up the corruption. So far it hasn't helped. Their cost-of-living gauge is the price of gari. The price had been 12 cups/shilling. Now they receive only five.

One casualty of the coup was the head customs official who chose suicide over surrender; but recently when we received the Christmas gifts mailed from the States in October, we were still charged $5 customs on a box valued at $4.

On their own initiative and entirely by their own efforts, Marty and Sara Jo had a benefit "fair" for the hospital with such things as a fish pond, puppet show, monster house, and Kool-Aid. At a penny a booth they cleared several shillings and provided a lot of fun for everyone.

I had planned to write as soon as we returned from our trip, but after a very dry dry-season, rains came and lightening knocked out our generator. The kids thought candles and kerosene lanterns were fun, but it was frustrating for me. At least we got to bed earlier. Tonight we have power thanks to a member of the church who manages an off-shore drilling company at Port Harcourt. He sent a generator from one of his rigs for our use until ours is repaired. Now I understand why civilization made so much progress after electricity.

Love,
Dit

April 1, 1966

Dear folks,

I'm sure every parent can empathize with me tonight as I breathe a sigh of relief that another April 1 is history. I had no idea before I came that April Fool's Day was so international even Nigeria was aware of it.

Henry was the kids' main target today. He receives stacks of job applications daily. So they composed one picking up on the usual style plus their own exaggerations. After an introduction of flowery admiration and confidence that Henry would not fail to help a brother in need, they concluded with a threat of suicide if the writer failed to get a job. Henry fell for it! "Just listen to this one! I can't believe it!" And he read it aloud at the dinner table while the kids looked smugly at one another. Then they let him have it, "April Fool!"

Hospital plans are progressing well. Green Lawn Church, Lubbock, Texas, has been collecting building funds. Nancy and Iris have begun their second class of trainees. The first does so well that Henry depends on them at the out-patient clinic. When you consider that these are local girls who grew up in mud huts on dirt floors with elementary educations learning nursing procedures and sterile technique, our "sister tutors" are to be congratulated.

Two nights ago Lee ran a splinter between his toes so deep that Henry had to inject novocaine and work for over an hour to remove it while Lee screamed the entire time. Everyone was exhausted. When the ordeal finally ended, Lee calmly said, "I'm glad my daddy is a doctor."

He's been our Dennis the Menace, our perpetual motion machine. Nigerians can't keep their hands off his shock of white hair -- maybe wondering if it's real. He has accidentally thrown a rock through Bryants' window. He has put ashes in Patti's wash water -- no accident there. He has climbed through their window from the outside leaving muddy tracks up a newly painted wall. With the help of David Bryant, he tore off part of the thatched playhouse roof. Then he gives me his disarming smile and says, "Mamma, you are my best friend." I preach, I punish, and I pray. Sometimes he seems just curious about what might happen. Other times it seems his actions get ahead of his reasoning. I'm just thankful we don't live next door to a Mr. Wilson.

Shopping for even the smallest item can take so much time and so much energy, I'm grateful for everything I brought; and I keep a list for the next one coming from America. When Marty broke the last plastic hairband she uses for her long straight hair, I walked through the market row by row, stall by stall, trying to describe what I was looking for. Eager for a sale and not having heard of such in their culture, they kept shoving other things in my face. Finally after a two and a half hour search, I found four for approx. $1.50 (10 cents each at Woolworths). I've never enjoyed shopping, even in America.

Before learning to keep film in the "fridge," Marty and I both broke the winding spools in our cameras trying to wind film stuck on the roll from the heat. We shop for film now in air-conditioned stores, but even then we can't depend on it. Who knows how much heat the film was exposed to in transport, and frequently it has been "spoiled."

So fresh film stays on our list. I've also found the "fridge" ideal for candy, gum, and lipstick.

We were so happy to receive an audiotape John Morgan made from his phone conversations with Mema and George. Visualizing them as we listened was almost like a visit.

This week we've been enjoying the Elvis Huffard family, who are here to see their daughter Joyce Harrison and Don at Ukpom. They were early missionaries here, and now the first from churches of Christ in Sierra Leone.

So many come and go from Tennessee and report to Henry's family that finally I am happy to say someone is going to Indiana. Keesees leave this month, and Ruth is from Palmyra, Indiana. You can be sure they have a map to the Johnson farm.

Love,
Dit

April 10, 1966

Dear folks,

What an exciting week! Word came that the new military governor of the Eastern Region, Lt. Col. Chukwuemeka Odumegwu Ojukwu, would be visiting Aba and driving past the hospital. Anticipating a stop, crowds from all the surrounding villages gathered at the hospital and lined the road with palm branches. One sewed a flag with the green-white-green stripes going horizontally instead of vertically. "It's still our flag," he insisted. Marty dressed in her Scout uniform. Rees prepared a gift copy of Dr. Mattox's book *The Eternal Kingdom* with a letter inside requesting a transformer for the hospital. NEPA (Nigerian Electric Power Authority) has a high voltage line along the road by the hospital, but they tell us that to hook onto it we must buy our own transformer at about $9000.

Excitement escalated with the approaching sirens. Then as suddenly as he appeared he was gone. Instead the motorcade was stopping at Nwaigwe Police station on the opposite hill. Rees jumped into his car. Marty and Lee climbed in with him. Others hopped on their cycles and pedaled hard down one hill and up the other.

Despite the huge crowd pressing around the governor, Rees was able to present the book and say, "Your Excellency, our prayers are with you." He responded, "Prayers are what we need most." He shook Marty's hand eyeing her uniform and ran his fingers through Lee's white hair (a gesture of curiosity that Nigerians, even a governor, can't resist). Marty took his photo but said later her hand was shaking so hard she wondered if she got him. She told us, "He's the kind of man you like immediately." Now Lee begins his prayers with the things most important to him, "Help Tigger (pet genet) and help the new military governor."

The carpenter made David an insect display case with a sliding glass top. He has most of his collection carefully labeled and keeps moth balls inside to protect them from ants, moths, and fungus. Don Harrison, who teaches biology at the Ukpom Secondary School has been so impressed that a ten-year-old could do such scientific work, he asked David to speak to his students and show his collection. For his presentation David made a chart of all the orders illustrating each with beautiful free-hand drawings -- if a bug could be called beautiful. He gave such an excellent talk we're all very proud of him.

On Friday the children decorated Easter eggs. Today, Easter, Marty and Sara Jo gave the younger kids a party planning it all by themselves. Marty baked a cake and shaped it like a bunny. They had games, favors, and a puppet show, but the egg hunt had to be indoors because of the rain.

With the word out that an American doctor is available, we have expatriate visitors almost daily -- missionaries from other groups, industrial workers, Peace Corp volunteers, etc. A Mennonite doctor with his wife, an R.N., and four children stopped yesterday. When they left, we went to have dinner with a Lutheran family. We enjoy much more fellowship here among the religious groups than we would in America, perhaps because we are all strangers in a foreign land battling a common enemy.

It has been interesting to me to learn how different sponsors support their workers. Some have salaries based on a cost-of-living index published in America. Some were told to include a year's supply of canned food in their shipment from America. Some are provided major appliances and some live off the land as closely as possible. Some have offered to pay me for the cost of the meal when I entertained them because that is the practice in their group.

One family we see frequently has been a Seventh Day Adventist family who have a teen-age daughter with no friend near and she enjoy Marty. We first met them when the father had almost fainted in the road that goes by the school and came to our house for a drink and to rest. It was a very hot Saturday, and he had been cycling for miles visiting their churches. Henry said he had to resist the temptation to tell him he wouldn't have felt ill if he had done only a Sabbath Day's journey. They are so frugal they came to Nigeria not by plane, but by accompanying their personal goods on a freighter. When they visit I cook vegetarian, but he was happy to bring us some American canned pork and beans he'd discovered in Aba. He and Henry have lively, but friendly, theological discussions.

How I wish I could enjoy the arrival of spring with you! Our only change of seasons is from wet to dry and back again.

Love,
Dit

April 20, 1966

Dear folks,

I have just finished making myself a muumuu. Paul says it's called that because it makes me look like a cow. In the tropics comfort takes precedence over appearance. This one is really an eyeful with black African dancers and masks on a background of bright orange and red. Henry took one look and exclaimed, "I hope you don't plan to wear that!" Now why else would I have made it? Remember the old saying, "When in Rome..." When I put it on, it was the first time I'd had Nigerians tell me what a beautiful dress I had. I even bought extra cloth for Marty.

If there is one section of the Aba market I could say I enjoyed, it would be the cloth department with its satins and brocades, colorful Java wax prints, tie-and-dyes in unique patterns, and hand woven cloth from Akwete with gleaming metallic threads. I keep wondering who has the money to afford all these. Someone does or they couldn't keep such a large stock on hand.

The Aba market is indescribable to anyone who has not seen a huge outdoor market, a labyrinth of packed stalls and narrow passageways. I might compare it to a horizontal department store that extends for blocks with sections for different commodities -- lumber, hardware, books, groceries, etc. I would never go there alone with my poor sense of direction. If my shopping companion should turn a corner so that I temporarily lose sight of her, all I have to do is ask, "Have you seen my sister?" There are so few white people, I am immediately told where to go.

You can capture the sounds of Nigeria on tape and the sights on camera, but nothing has yet been invented that can capture the smells. In the market they are concentrated -- the odor of indigo in the cloth section, the blend of freshly cut wood and open sewers in the lumber section, and in the food section the smells of acrid palm oil, fermenting gari, and overpowering dried imported stockfish like dead fish. They tell me that it doesn't taste at all like it smells. To one who has been nurtured on it the aroma is that of real home-cooking.

Once I inadvertently wandered into the area where they were grinding red hot peppers. Before I could retreat, I went into spasms of sneezing, snorting, and coughing to the delight of all the observers. One day when Lee went with me, I glanced back to be sure he was following. He was -- with his thumb and forefinger clamped tightly over his nose.

I think it is important to involve the children in the work as much as possible. Recently we received 100 lb. bags of crushed wheat and dry milk from U.S. AID. Inside the large bags were small ones stamped, "Donated by the people of the United States of America. Not for sale or exchange." I set up an assembly line with the kids to package it for distribution at the clinic. Even Hank and Lee enjoyed trotting back and forth between the "fillers' and the "tiers" with first an empty bag then a full one. The children were really happy to have helped in a valuable work for the hospital. Now, I just hope it will reach the malnourished children we see and not be sold by the adults to buy gari that only fills the belly.

Sunday night we were treated to an amazing display of the Aurora Australis (Southern lights). At least that's what I thought it was because it looked just like the Northern lights I used to see in Indiana. If so, it would indeed have been a rare occurrence considering we are about 5 degrees north of the Equator. The Nigerians watching with us had never seen anything like it before, nor even heard of such. Red streaks shot high into the sky above an arc of glowing red and yellow. Some thought the Russians or Shell Oil might be doing something. Others were just plain scared.

Monday I was sewing when I heard Rees yell, "Come quick!" I dashed to the front door and saw him holding Lee in the car with blood streaming down Lee's face. I jumped in the car, made pressure on the wound, and we took off for the clinic. Rees explained that Lee had hit his head on the sharp corner of a metal window frame that cranked outward. At the clinic, I began washing his face keeping up the pressure until I finally came to the cut. By then the bleeding had stopped and I discovered that the cut was so small it didn't even need one stitch. Lee is always full of surprises.

Because we sponsor Monday John at the secondary school, they sent us his grades. This first period he was first out of sixty classmates. We knew he could do it!

The Underwoods have just returned from an Obudu vacation. I've kidded them that I'd be disappointed if no one got sick. Patti Bryant has been receiving emetine treatments for amoebiasis following their trip there.

Love,
Dit

May 4, 1966

Dear folks,

We are well into rainy season, but so far most of the rain has been going around us leaving us with only the high humidity. I stay bathed in sweat because the air is so saturated it can't evaporate.

Hank's eighth birthday was Saturday. He'd wanted a swimming party, but he's had a cold, Lee's on penicillin for a sore throat, and David's had a measles-like rash with a low grade fever (cause unknown). So we had his friends in for his favorite meal -- ground nut stew and birthday cake.

Recently Ray and Charlotte Lanham arrived to work wherever needed. Every house on the Bible School campus is occupied, so they have been living at Ukpom while Ray commutes to build their house, the first residence to go up on hospital property. They moved in on Monday, and last night we welcomed them with a "pounding." Ray will supervise the construction of the maternity and kitchen/laundry. Rees is overseeing the work on a large ward and the operating room. David saw the hospital plans and excitedly told all the kids, "We're going to have movies at the hospital!" He'd seen the word "theatre" and didn't know it was British for the operating room.

Hank and Lee now boast every kid's dream -- a secret hideout. Only theirs is a bit different -- an abandoned white ant hill. Some hills are eight feet high. This is a tall one as large around as it is high -- big enough to scoop out a cave that can hide both of them and their treasures. And it's cool inside!

Because the early rains have been so spasmodic, I've had to replant my garden, and so have the Nigerians. But there is a big difference. Mine is important to me for the exercise after a day indoors because of the heat and school. Theirs is their livelihood. For the past two weeks we've been enjoying fresh corn-on-the-cob from my garden and sweet green peppers which I've not found in markets here. Africans like the hot chilies. I also have a watermelon a foot long and a bed of fresh lettuce. I plant lettuce the year round and pick only the outside leaves to keep it bearing for months. The Bibb variety seems to do best.

Patti and I learned that there would be an eclipse. We prepared boxes for the kids to put over their heads with a pinhole in back and white paper inside the front so they could watch the action without damaging their eyes. As the sky darkened all the kids lined up on the front walk with boxes over their heads. The Nigerians passing along the road in front stopped to stare. I wondered if they might be thinking this was some kind of "white man" ritual to restore the fading sun. Just to be on the safe side with our workers, I asked them to look in a box for themselves, and they were astonished. They should pass on their discovery.

We've found a good public library at Ikot Ekpene that will allow us to check out books. They've even offered to bring their bookmobile by the school so that the Bible students can also use it.

Tomorrow will be an exciting day. We plan to go to Port Harcourt to meet Roger Church and V.M. Whitesell, coming loaded like Santa.

Love,
Dit

May 17, 1966

Dear folks,

Last week David Underwood suffered what appeared to be a light heart attack. He's at Queen Elizabeth Hospital, Umuahia, with Henry going to check on him daily. But David's not so sure he'll be better off staying the three weeks they recommend. He says that the man on one side of him is raving and uncontrollable with rabies while the one on the other side coughs incessantly from tuberculosis.

I can hear Marty and Sara Jo giggling as they work on origami storks. They read that the Japanese consider origami storks a symbol of wishes for good health and that 1000 will assure recovery. They made a mobile of 1000 for Patti when she was confined to bed for amoebiasis treatment. Now that she's feeling great, they are working on another 1000 for David Underwood. (It gets a little confusing at times with four Davids on campus.)

The kids finish schoolwork easily in the mornings but are never at a loss in the afternoons. Paul has his books and David his bugs. With access to a new library Henry has been trying to persuade David to read about something besides insects. Marty has worked diligently to complete Junior badges before she becomes a Cadet Scout. At last count she had earned 25 plus the Signs of the Arrow and Star. Hank and Lee prefer soccer ("football" here), and there always seems to be plenty Nigerian kids around to join in once they start a game. It's fun to watch them, like acrobats, bounce the ball off any part of their bodies, even their heads.

Clinic attendance is gaining momentum. Usually Henry goes up (it is on a hill) at 7:30 for a devotional with the workers before seeing patients. He returns home at noon for lunch and a brief rest. At noon he said of the 250 registered today (Wednesday), he will try to see the most ill leaving at least 100 to receive numbers for Friday's clinic, though most have walked or cycled for miles. Even the 150/day average allows him only about three minutes each -- certainly not ideal, but better than no medical care at all, which they had before he came.

A few days ago we had to tell the workers there was no more money to buy cement, and block-making came to a halt. But every time that happens, funds suddenly appear from some unexpected source, and we keep going and hoping. Our regional Minister of Health from Enugu came by Tuesday to inspect the work and said we had his permission to open whenever we thought we were ready, and he would look forward to attending the opening ceremonies.

Roger Church, V.M. Whitesell, and Copeland Baker left yesterday. Lucien Palmer, one of the earlier missionaries here and now president of Michigan Christian College, also came. These four, members of the board for the Nigerian Christian Schools, were finally able to get the deed for school property at Ukpom officially signed over to the board this week. It had been promised in front of a lawyer, and already the school has been in operation for two years with buildings in which they have invested thousands of dollars. We have been concerned because it wasn't on paper. I heard that the hold-up had been a prominent polygamist with strong political ambitions, now unappreciated by the new government. So far the only complaints I have heard about the new military government have been from displaced politicians.

The visitors brought so much for the missionaries, they were 50 lbs. overweight but somehow managed to get it all in without paying an extra cent. The Nigerian men wear mesh "singlet" undershirts. I've not been able to find the knit sleeveless kind Henry likes. When V.M. was ready to leave, I asked him if I might buy his. Instead he insisted on a trade. So he left with huge holes showing from beneath his lovely white shirt saying proudly it was a tribute to Henry's service. And they still planned to go by Liberia and Sierra Leone before reaching Nashville.

May 21: I've been so busy helping Marty get out her campus newspaper to complete her writer's badge that I didn't get my letter off. Now I'm so tired it's hard to write.

Today I went with the three Girl Scouts on their second all day hike. (Iris Hays and Charlotte Lanham helped with the first.) I'm sure no other troop has ever had a hike quite like ours. At 6:30 a.m. we cooked breakfast outdoors over the buddy burners we had made earlier. For those unfamiliar with Scout lingo, a buddy burner is made by removing one end of a gallon size can then punching vent holes. It is inverted over a small flat can like a tuna can that has been filled with rolled corrugated cardboard which is then saturated with melted paraffin for instant fuel. It produces a quick high heat ideal for frying bacon and eggs and toasting bread using the top of the can as a pan -- nothing to scrub.

We began walking toward the village of Onicha Ngwa, an area so thickly populated that the only nature study we were able to do was human nature. Every move we made was so intensely interesting to them that they stared at us and discussed us among themselves in Ibo as if we were not present. At rest stops we were surrounded by both adults and children. They wanted to know where we were going and if they might help. Every day they will walk for miles, but to walk just for the sake of walking! Leave it to the crazy Americans to think up that one!

We were followed by such a long trail of naked kids I felt like Pied Piper. At each compound we passed more streamed out yelling "Becca! Becca!" like heralds announcing royalty, then they too joined the happy procession.

We came to the stream where some were beating out clothes on a log, some were washing vegetables and soaking cassava, and others bathing and just playing. It was such a lovely stream and such a typical scene I wanted a photo. With all the chatting about us in Ibo, I assumed that no one understood English. I motioned to my camera. Immediately one lady straightened up and said plainly, "Give me money." Having none with me I solved the problem by posing the girls beside the stream and guess what -- the villagers just happened to be in the background.

The Scout manual specified a cookout as part of the hike so we returned to the campus barbecue pit. I didn't relish an audience over every bite. Remember this is rainy season and to paraphrase an old classic: Wet wood does not a good fire make! Somehow the Nigerians manage that one too. Also I learned that Nigerian beef sliced thin and pounded with meat tenderizer is still not ideal for dry heat. After a brief struggle with stringy beef, half-done potatoes, and doughy doughboys, we fudged and went to the house for peanut butter sandwiches.

The day was so hot we rested briefly before taking off again -- this time for Nlagu, the village on the other side of the highway. We met a man descending a ladder he'd made from a single bamboo pole with the stubs of branches as foot rests. He held a calabash of palm wine freshly tapped from the top of the tree. The fresh is rare. Fermentation doesn't take long in this heat. Curious to taste what the locals crave, I motioned to my cup and he generously poured some. One taste was enough! I took the rest home for others to sample. To my surprise no one else had enough curiosity to get closer than the smell. In fact Nancy Petty declared, "That Grace Farrar and John Beckloff would eat anything!"

John, our washerman had begged me "Come see my place (Nlagu)." News travels fast. Soon he appeared and was so happy to see us he asked to be our guide. He pointed out a plant that was to became the most fascinating part of the hike. Whenever it was touched it immediately shriveled as if dead, then shortly restored itself. The girls labeled it "die plant."

I would really enjoy a nature study with the kids if only I could find the identification books. When I ask the villagers, "What do you call that?" I get the general Ibo name for tree, bird, etc. Apparently their curiosity takes them no further, so they wonder why should mine.

It was a market day bustling with all the usual trading. Suddenly we heard music, and a lady came through the crowd dancing and holding high a placard with a man's picture followed by a band and family members. John explained that she was celebrating the tenth anniversary of her husband's death. They feel that the spirit of the deceased is with them active in their current affairs. The memorial celebrations are to assure that the spirit will be pleased and bring them good, not evil. We made a quick exit so that our presence would not detract from her celebration.

Marty and Sara Jo have been dreaming up a costume birthday party for Marty's (today) and Sara's (June 1). We've decided to postpone it until David Underwood is out of the hospital and Becky will be free from baby-sitting for Brian. Instead we had cake at home and opened family gifts. It always amazes me what the kids can come up with when shopping is so limited. The most original was Lee's. He had made a book of his original crayola drawings. One page had a big round head with a long, long neck and the rest of the page was colored green. His interpretation: "That's me in bed with my favorite green sheets and just my head sticking out."

Tonight Lee suddenly told me, "Mama, I like God, but I don't like church. All I do is put in money, and they never give me anything to eat."

Love,
Dit

June 11, 1966

Dear folks,

Surely God is the sponsor of the hospital! Today we dismissed all the construction crew with "Money done finish," and we had no idea when we might have more. Tonight when we opened our mail from Aba there was $5000! -- $2000 from Brother F.F. Carson's congregation in Richmond, California, and $3000 from West End church, Nashville, in response to the reports given by Roger Church and others who had been here.

Today the women came -- volunteers from local churches -- walking, cycling, and carrying machetes. They spent the day clearing the land, cutting grass, and digging up stumps -- singing all the while. After a full day of hard labor, they went home walking or cycling, some as far as ten miles, to prepare meals for their families.

Would American women ever have equaled that desire to have a hospital? I wondered. Personally I wouldn't have had the energy. I hate to admit I was not there working with them, but I would probably have cut my leg off with the machete. Actually I was at the house finishing one school year to begin a new one in two days. I'm timing this school year to end by early spring next year to give us time to prepare for our homeward journey.

Last Saturday was the monthly all-day ladies' fellowship. I'd observed that the women and children's classes in local churches are still being taught by the men. The women have a great deal more confidence with a machete than a Bible class. Why? Do they feel a lack of ability, or do the men insist that all teaching in the church is their job? Women do have considerable influence in village affairs, especially in the market, and villages have a separate women's organization.

To encourage the women to teach, I showed ways to teach children using what they have on hand, such as scratching stick figures in the sand and object lessons from common things. Becky and Marty did a Bible story with their home-made puppets. Having never seen anything like this before, the women cheered until the interpreter had to quieten them before the girls could finish. What a joy to teach here!

Today Moses Opara, our Nigerian missionary in the Muslim North, returned with his family -- or what was left of them. During a worship service at their building in Gusau, a band of Muslims burst in demanding, "Is the name of Allah known here?" Moses answered boldly, "The name of Jesus Christ is known here." The response was, "Kill them all!"

The Christians fled for their lives, but not before his youngest, about a year old, was bashed against the wall and killed. A kind Muslim lady hid them in her house from the mob at the risk of her own life. All his property was looted and burned. He himself escaped with only his underpants. When she could, the lady sneaked them out, and the police put them on a train going south. He said his shirt and pants, and even his wife's dress, were given to them by someone at the train station.

They came bruised, exhausted, and hungry, not having eaten in days. I boiled eggs, set out bread and peanut butter and everything I thought might taste good to a Nigerian. Even as he sat there, he kept repeating, "I must go back. You cannot change a nation until you change its spirit. They must be taught."

Moses has been preaching at Gusau, about 850 miles north of us on the south edge of the Sahara, for almost three years. He was truly a foreigner, often looked down on by the local people; yet he learned the Hausa language. Although Islam is the predominate religion there and to convert to Christianity may be life-threatening both to him and the convert, Moses had established a congregation of thirty-five Christians.

Moses understood what is was like to "go against the grain." He himself had been a ju-ju priest and a polygamist. He told us that the first time he heard Christianity preached in a market place he recognized the truth and trembled when he thought about the things he had done. He told how he had accepted pay to put a hex on someone, and then he would make sure that the person was poisoned so that people would say, "When Moses puts the hex on you, it works!"

Immediately after his own conversion he began teaching his landlord and those around him. When he heard Marshall Keeble preach, he is quoted as having said, " If he can preach at eighty-two, I can preach at thirty-two." Moses graduated from the Onicha Ngwa Bible College then chose the most difficult area in Nigeria as his mission field.

Marty and Sara had their costume party, and the children came as storybook characters. Paul was very creative as Puddleglum from Chronicles of Narnia with his pool flippers.

It's 8 p.m. Hard rain on the "zinc" above is music to me, reminiscent of my childhood. This will be a cooler night for sleeping.

Like magic, a brown land has suddenly become lush green. I have beautiful roses, daisies, crocus, cannas, and mums from my labors. And we've even had several watermelons from my vines!

Love,
Dit

June 26, 1966

Dear folks,

It's Sun. a.m. Henry has gone preaching with Paul. I like to go as much as possible, but I had no time during the week to prepare for my Sunday children's class. Last Sunday we all accompanied him to a remote area about 85 miles away leaving at 8 a.m., taking our lunch, and returning at 3 p.m. just in time for my class. What a day! Then Henry preached for the 4 p.m. campus service, and afterward Port Harcourt friends had supper with us.

Yesterday we spent all day in Port Harcourt meeting every plane from Lagos hoping to see Dr. Joe Mattox and Jim Massey who were scheduled to arrive in Lagos Friday. For some reason they didn't come, so Bryants have returned to the airport today. How often have we wished for a phone! Dr. Mattox is coming to see his sister, Patti Bryant, and her family and to give Henry a break. Jim is coming to prepare for about 35 evangelists he's expecting to arrive about July 8 for a five-week campaign.

With the recent windfall of funds, our maternity ward has been completed; a large women/children's ward lacks only the painting and the paint has been purchased; the kitchen/laundry is almost finished; and the footings have been poured for the surgery/x-ray building. We still need funds for the beds and equipment before we can open. Mrs. F.W. (Mildred) Mattox of Lubbock, Texas, has been phoning and writing friends for $35 each to buy a bed. So far she's had twenty donations.

The native doctors ("witch doctors") do a very active business and charge fees far exceeding ours. They always have the finest houses in a village except perhaps for the chief. Many people in our area, not educated about the causes of disease, think that the germs we talk about apply only to the white man's illnesses and that we really don't understand theirs, which they believe are caused by a spirit. Often our clinic is the last resort. The native doctor usually makes razor cuts on the affected part (we think to let the evil spirits out). Many who don't really understand what a doctor is supposed to do are not happy with their treatment unless they receive an injection -- any kind. Fortunately there has been so little exposure to antibiotics here that penicillin still works wonders for most bacterial infections. Some think they recover because the white man's ju-ju is stronger than a black man's ju-ju.

Every clinic day brings pathetic cases that have first received treatment from the native doctor. On our last clinic day parents brought in their three-year-old with a severe foot infection. The native doctor had made a series of slashes very close together on her foot and the infection had spread to every cut. Her foot was swollen so badly the skin was coming off. She will now need weeks of antibiotics followed by skin grafting. Now, will they stop coming once they begin to see an improvement? Many do thinking recovery will continue and never receive the full course for a complete cure. Also treatments cost them farming time and money. As a result they often end up worse. That's one way confinement in a hospital would help.

As an illustration of their belief in the supernatural power of an injection, we heard of a young man with no complaints who persuaded someone to give him an injection in his thigh simply because he had never had one. He ended up with an infection from a dirty needle that eventually cost him his leg.

Henry now sees about 170 patients on clinic days and another 30 come for injections and treatments given by the nurses. Rees has been trying to persuade immigration in Lagos to increase our missionary quota. Our medical work will help. Many newly independent African nations now insist that only those missionaries who also make a medical or educational contribution be allowed. The Catholics here have the best hospitals and biggest schools -- and an unrestricted quota.

In fact we were able to take advantage of the Catholic hospital at Anua having a nun ophthalmologist last week. We took Hank because he has been complaining of headaches and squinting when he reads. Now he will have glasses for astigmatism.

Paul has sent off his first lesson for the University of Nebraska High School and is doing better work this year because he finds it more interesting. It's a challenge for me too, especially algebra after not having given it a thought for over twenty-five years. Even though the courses are directed to the student, I want to be prepared for any questions. If we are fortunate the lessons will arrive in Lincoln, Nebraska, in three to six weeks, and it will take equally as long to receive an answer from his teacher there. In the meantime who know what may depend on that unanswered question.

Love,
Dit

Sun. p.m.   Bryants have returned with Jim and Joe. Besides instruments, Joe brought $1500 for the hospital.

July 22, 1966

Dear folks,

Thanks to Dr. Joe Mattox we had a short, but relaxing, vacation in Jos, though the trip home almost undid it. We've been home for about a week, but I've been too busy to write. I'd scarcely set foot on campus till I received a typical Jim Massey greeting, "Grace, I've got a job for you."

Jim, a good friend from Harding days, worked here until a few months before we came. I really appreciate him, but I'm a marathoner not a sprinter. Opportunities here seem limited only by time and energy, and I soon discovered I had a very finite amount of both. As Henry describes his medical part, "It's like trying to dip the ocean dry with a teaspoon." So I had no qualms of conscience answering, "Sorry, Jim, I'm already booked."

David Underwood suffered indigestion-like pains all night, but didn't tell Henry until this afternoon when the pain became more severe. Henry sent him back to Queen Elizabeth Hospital at Umahia and went to see about him as soon as he could close the clinic. We're still waiting on Henry's report.

Henry and Dr. Mattox both felt that David should make plans to return to America where better medical care is available -- another loss for the mission and the missionaries! We're just getting to know them. David could even persuade Henry to take a little recreation time. When Henry came home from work, David would stick his head out their back door and yell, "Emergency" -- their code word for a chess game.

There was so much to see and do in Jos I can touch only the highlights. First, the climate was so like America that, now back, Henry said he felt as if he were returning for a third tour. (He made a brief survey alone in '63.) Jos is on a plateau surrounded by hills and rocks left by ancient glaciers. One the kids especially enjoyed climbing was "Camel Rock," silhouetted like a resting camel. The temperature was warm enough to swim in the afternoon, but cool enough to use the fireplace at night.

We stayed at the SIM (Sudan Interior Mission) rest house where American food with an abundance of good fresh vegetables grown locally cost less than feeding the family at Onich Ngwa. There are about 600 SIM missionaries in Nigeria alone. Guests from many denominations and from many West African countries were also vacationing there. Just visiting them and listening to their stories made the trip worthwhile for me.

The kids especially liked the zoo featuring African animals. Four chimps performed for peanuts, so the kids gave them peanuts one by one to keep the show going. One lioness never moved her eyes off Lee. Whenever he came near her cage, she made a lunge. I was so thankful for the bars.

Especially interesting to me was a museum of Nigerian art and antiquities with a library of Nigerian history. Maps made by early explorers showed how little they really knew about Africa.

We toured a pottery where Henry even tried his hand at the potter's wheel. The teacup he tried to shape was salvaged by the potter to become a sugar bowl. Since the glazing, firing, etc. would be a two-week process, the potter just gave us a lump of clay to play with at home, and the kids chose souvenirs.

One day we ate at a museum/restaurant said to be a replica of the house of an ancient Benin king. We also visited a tin smelting plant, a dairy, and a veterinary research center. Since our area cannot have cattle because of the tsetse fly that carries African sleeping sickness, it was a rare treat for the children to have fresh milk every day. I insisted on taking a photo of a beautiful holstein herd grazing in a lush green pasture. Henry asked why I would waste film on a scene that looked exactly like America. I told him that was precisely the point. No one would believe this was Africa.

At the milk processing plant they were also mixing dried milk with peanut flour, another product of the North, for UNICEF to distribute to hospitals. (Protein deficiency is a major health problem in Nigeria.) I brought some home to try.

A snake charmer appeared on the street one day and charmed us as well. He had cobras, hoods spread, weaving all around his body and even put one in his mouth. He let them bite his arms in several places, then for about $1.50/packet tried to sell a black powder he claimed made him immune to their poison. I wanted Henry to get some for analysis; but he said that there's no cure and the man had probably milked them before his show. The man wrapped a cobra so the head was inside the body coils and passed it around so the children could say they'd handled a live cobra.

The return trip was almost as exciting as the vacation. Henry estimated it should be a six-hour trip if we drove straight home and snacked along the way -- usually on bananas and peanuts. We had stopped at the Makurdi and Enugu rest houses going to Jos but had long waits for food service. Anyway, I never felt comfortable about the food safety, after having once seen a sausage ball roll off a counter tray and across the floor only to be retrieved and replaced without even a casual brushing off.

We left Jos at 5:30 a.m. and drove gingerly over numerous narrow bridges and unpaved roads that had received a few shovel tosses of dirt for a rainy season quick-fix. The fills had changed into slippery mud. Former tarmac was now tire-rending rocks. We seemed to be in constant danger of either sliding off the road into the mud or having the tires slashed miles from nowhere. We reached Makurdi and paved roads about noon and Enugu in three more hours. Then detour signs for a washed-out bridge sent us to Onitcha, more than fifty miles out of our way.

Onitcha, Eastern Nigeria's largest city, was a new experience for us. In the distance we saw the new bridge arching the Niger River, the only one of its kind in Nigeria. Suddenly we were on a smooth, wide highway exclaiming, "This looks just like an American superhighway!" When "what to our wondering eyes should appear" but a big red hexagonal "Stop," instead of the usual British "Halt," and we all had a good laugh. We'd heard about USAID building a superhighway across the nation.

After almost fifteen hours on the road, it was 8:15 p.m. when we reached the campus. All the families came pouring out to welcome us with all kinds of exciting news; Patti had dinner waiting; and there was a big stack of mail. After our longest, most difficult drive, what a relief to be back!

Early the next morning Joe Mattox left for Tanzania. So with no chance to rest from his "rest," Henry had clinic. He was very happy to have Matt Young (son of M. Norvel and Helen), who came with the evangelists, helping. Although Matt is still pre-med, Joe has taught him how to draw blood and other medical skills.

Saturday J.R. Lewis, manager of the International Drilling Co., Port Harcourt, came with his oil drilling rig and crew to give us a well. It was 4 p.m. before they could set up. At 107 feet they found water. It was after midnight when they put down the pipe. Henry stayed with them and brought them supper and coffee. After the others were in bed, Paul and I went up to watch until they finished. The men insisted on returning to P.H. that night. After only a couple hours' of sleep, they were back at 7 a.m. to drill a second well, but instead discovered that the first had stopped up and worked most of the day with it. They said they should have pumped it clean the night before. They're hoping to return this week-end and have it in full operation.

J.R. is a Christian who arrived last fall and has come from Port Harcourt every Sunday except for trouble-shooting on a rig once. Two others who worked with him are not members of the church but attend regularly. Not only is he donating the expense of bringing a rig from Port Harcourt and paying his crew overtime, but also he, usually in an office, did a lot of the hard labor himself -- a job others had estimated at $3000.

The 32 evangelists Jim Massey brought scattered to Aba, Ukpom, and Enugu preaching daily in towns, markets, and churches. Fifteen are staying in the Aba rest house. Wednesday night they appeared with ten pounds of ground beef, bread, and all the trimmings for a burger feast saying they were tired of British food. Could our cook make good old American hamburgers? He could and did -- a picnic for us all! One of the group had a bad leg infection from a previous injury. Henry ordered antibiotics, resting the leg for a week, and hot packs; so he moved to Bryants for Patti to nurse. He joked that others will get sore legs to have good American meals.

Two women came with the group -- David Underwood's mother, who came to visit and help the family, and Bonnie Beaver, a home economics teacher from Freed Hardeman. Bonnie has had daily classes for several village women on health, nutrition, sewing, and Bible. They each made a personal dress pattern and sewed a dress.

The chief was so appreciative he made a special trip to the compound trying to persuade someone to continue classes for other women. Sorry, we're all booked.

Love,
Dit

"Because It Is Our Custom, Madam"

I set about to explore Africa as "full of 'satiable curtiosity" as Kipling's Elephant Child and asking "ever so many questions."

My queries were met mostly with amusement as if to say, "Don't you know?" or "How could there be any other way?" And the answer was usually, "Because it is our custom, Madam." If I did get a real answer, I knew the Ibo might let his desire to say what he thought I wanted to hear take precedence over the truth, not to deceive but to please.

When a villager built his house near our compound, I was excited for the opportunity to observe every step of the process. I watched as he anchored poles in the ground for the framework of a rectangular house, crossed those with bamboo, then bound it all tightly together with tie-tie, a kind of vine rope. I watched him dig a hole, carry water, and trample the dirt into mud to be plastered into the frame ---asking question all the time. Finally he turned to me with an amused smile and said, "Tell me, Madam, just how do they build them in your country?" No more comments or questions from me!

Historically Iboland was isolated by water -- the Niger River on the west, the Benue to the north, the Cross River on the east, and the Atlantic to the south. Inland the dense tropical rain forrest separated villages until the advent of motor vehicles opened roads. From this isolation customs, rituals, and even the language developed in many different ways. Even the translation of the Bible itself was delayed, after it had been translated for other major tribes, by disagreements about which Ibo (or Igbo) dialect to use.

I searched market stalls and bookstores for any thing I could find on Ibo history and culture. I learned there were no written records of early Ibo history. In fact no one knew where the name itself came from, perhaps some family lost to history. The Ibos of the area where we lived are referred to as the "Ngwa people." I was told that the word "Ngwa" meant "quick." Why were they called "quick people?"

Depending on whom you asked, some said, "quick to anger, quick to kill, volatile;" while others said, " quick to learn, quick to act, energetic, intelligent."

The Ibo was never one to stay home and wait for opportunity to come to him. Families and even villages sometimes combined their resources to send a promising young person away for an education expecting him in return to help those who had helped him. Ibos will be found all over West Africa and also in European nations and America working and training to improve their lot and help their extended families. Very few areas have not been changed by this exposure to Western culture. With so many variations in rituals, tabus, customs, etc., and even those rapidly changing with education and outside influences, I can only briefly touch on some of the practices that most affected our work.

A major problem in the church was polygamy. We never wavered from the Biblical teaching "one man, one woman" as the will of God. Local churches disfellowshipped those who refused to give up extra wives and those who took another wife after becoming Christians. For women believers caught up in polygamy it was more difficult. They could not go out and find a job; nor could women without a man have land to farm for their children; their families did not want them back with the possibility of having to return the bride price; and few men would want a wife that had left her first husband.

The government allowed the registration of only one legal wife to protect her rights. In the eyes of the people the couple were considered married when they held the traditional ceremony with the exchange of gifts, but we encouraged the people to register their marriages. Polygamy continues to be a dying practice as people want better health and education for their children, fewer laborers are needed to work decreasing farm land, and the plurality of wives as a symbol of wealth and status is being replaced by such Western goals as education and material possessions.

"Bride price" is another custom the government has tried to regulate by setting a maximum, but it has not been successful. A poor man may have to postpone his marriage for many years and still end up indebted for many more. Somehow most do reach a final stage of negotiations. Sometimes the "bride" is still a child, and the husband agrees to pay her school fees. I knew of parents who were so happy their daughter chose a Christian, though he had no money, they told him, "Forget the bride price." I knew of another whose son married overseas, and they were so embarrassed that he hadn't paid anything for his wife that they gave her gifts for her to give her parents saying, "Don't ever say that you didn't cost anything." The young wife of one of my workers was so unhappy in her marriage she ran back to her family. He came to me moaning, "My money! My money!"

Jesus' admonition that a man should leave his parents and "cleave" to his wife is contrary to Ibo tradition. The wife is assimilated into the man's family. Friendship with brothers and other men is considered more important than a man's relationship with his wife, who is generally considered his property. Seldom was any affection for a wife expressed publicly, but it was not uncommon to see two men walking down the street holding hands in friendship. That too is changing with Western influence. One Christian man explaining to me why his relationship with his mother was more important to him than with his wife said, "Your wife may leave you, but your mother never will."

Funeral feasts also incurred heavy debts. In the high heat and humidity without the benefit of embalming, the burial of a corpse was usually the same day as the death in a simple wooden casket usually in the floor of the house or on the compound. A ceremony and feast according to the person's status came later when there had been time to make the proper arrangements. Butchering a cow, providing copious amounts of palm wine, hiring a band and dancers were all a heavy financial burden on the poor. The spirit of the deceased, believed by heathen to be hovering around partaking in the ceremonies, could thus be sent off happily. Until this ceremony took place, the spirit was considered homeless inside the hut or compound. Eventually it would return and take a definite interest in family affairs.

I asked one Christian begging for financial help why he would go into debt for his deceased mother if he did not believe what the customs represented. He answered, "The people expect it, Madam. If I don't kill a cow, they will carry off the door to my house and do all kinds of bad things to me." It is hard for us to understand the social pressures that Christians undergo from their unbelieving families and villages. But we held consistently to rules: "NO money for bride price." "NO money for funeral feasts."

The Ibos recognized two kinds of doctors or "dibia," both of which they considered legitimate -- "dibia afa" (doctor of charms, "witch doctor," or native doctor) and "dibia ogwu" (doctor of medicine). Even some of our Bible teachers saw nothing wrong in resorting to the "dibia afa" at times. Henry said he could tell the major complaint before he asked by the cuts over the affected part. The native doctor dealt with spirits, charms, local herbs, etc. often requiring sacrifices to appease a vengeful spirit, and often more expensive than medical fees.

The Ibos place such a high value on courtesy, that they never carry out any conversation or correspondence before expressing proper greetings, asking about the state of one's health and that of his family. Again when departing, good-byes include wishing the other a safe journey and God's blessings to go with him. A gift is offered and received with both hands implying that one's whole self is involved. The Ibo handshake may be of three parts -- grasping the palm, changing to the thumbs, and sliding off with a snap -- or may be pressing fingertips firmly, then withdrawing quickly to produce a snap.

One of the most important parts of every social ceremony among the Ibo is sharing a kola-nut. It serves as a token of good will among friends and a welcome to visitors. The ceremony may vary with the occasion, the number of people involved, etc., but essentially the host who provided the nut offers it on a plate (sometimes with a knife for cutting depending on the size of the nut and the number of people) first to the visitor for him to give thanks for the nut and pray for the well being of the host. The visitor then separates, or cuts, the nut as his special privilege. The plate is next presented to the host, who with a wave of his hand indicates that the visitor should first partake. After doing so, the visitor passes it on to the youngest and so it goes person by person to the eldest who next partakes. After which the others share the nut. Henry delighted them by learning the appropriate Ibo words for the kola ceremony.

In our area a long red pepper called "alligator pepper" was frequently served as an accompaniment to the kola. At social events a tray of "garden eggs" (a small, round, hard, bitter vegetable) and "minerals" (individual bottles of carbonated beverages) were usually served after the kola ceremony.

An Ibo man once said, "It is difficult to explain to an European the importance of the kola nut to the Ibo." They were always quick to forgive us for any breach in etiquette from our lack of understanding and equally as quick to point out our error.

Henry once as a host in Western style courtesy ("ladies first") offered the kola nut to me to cut. The Nigerian immediately interrupted, "Women never cut the kola!" -- as I saw it, revealing both the value placed on the kola and on women. The old school of thought would not have allowed them to partake either, but in mixed gatherings I was often offered the kola. My first taste of one was so bitter I could barely conceal an involuntary shudder. On the next occasion, I politely said, "No, thank you," in the way I had taught my children to refuse food. I was rebuked, "You never say 'no' to the kola!" After that I scraped my teeth across it as a "no thank you helping" then discreetly dropped the remainder down into my dress for retrieval later. If an Ibo reads this he will forgive me for, after all, I am only a woman.

The kola nut is found in the seed pod of a tropical tree, Cola Acuminata, and is easily separated into sections. Colors may vary from white to red. Containing caffeine, it was an original ingredient in the American cola drinks. Although bitter tasting, it was prized by the older people who chewed it to prevent hunger pangs in times of food shortages or on long journeys. Perhaps because it gives a feeling of renewed energy, the Ibos have a saying, "He who bring kola, brings life."

Farrar Family Album

Our Home
(1964-1967)

"Like father, like son", Hank & Henry (1965)

Grace Farrar preparing to teach a class of hospital trainees. Note snow picture which helped to keep us cool. (1965)

David Farrar playing with an Enugu Zoo python (1966)

Hank & Lee were water carriers in training ▶

◀ Hank & Lee found in their secret hideout, a giant, deserted ant hill. (1965)

▲ Grace seen holding her famous home grown watermellon which was a first in the area thus proving it could be done. (1965)

Marty caring for their pet genet. (1965)

Paul holding the family genet (1966)

Our Third Year
1966 - 1967

Nigerian Christian Hospital (1967)

Missionaries' Children

◀ Lee & Hank Farrar help Becky Underwood bag dry milk from USAID for distribution in the clinic.

▲ Girl Scout Troop on Foreign Soil #2 in Nigeria: Becky Underwood, Marty Farrar & Sara Jo Bryant

Bible Class preschoolers were (l-r, front) Hank Farrar, Tonya Keesee, Becki Bryant, Lee Farrar, Dita Keesee & David Bryant. Teachers Marty Farrar & Sara Jo Bryant, standing in the back of the room, enjoyed teaching everyone.

Sunday, August 7, 1966

Dear folks,

I can only wonder what you may be hearing in America about the Nigerian political situation. I can be sure that reporters will try to make it seem as bad as possible. When the visitors left three days ago, we all wrote quick notes to our families to be mailed once they were outside of the country. I presume you've already received ours. Lagos continues to have the same old tribal conflicts, but our area is calm.

The most important news for us was David's baptism last Sunday evening. David himself has been bringing up the subject for months, but since he is only ten, Henry wondered if he understood. Finally David on his own initiative went to discuss it with Rees. After that we all gathered at the stream below the school where Marty was baptized two years ago, and Rees immersed David into the Lord. What joy to now have three children join us in the Lord's family!

Because of the turmoil in Lagos, domestic flights to Port Harcourt had been discontinued, so the evangelists chartered a taxi to Lagos. Becky Underwood returned with her grandmother to begin the school year in America. Marty, especially, will miss her. The night before she left Becky, along with Marty and Sara Jo, entertained us all with a two-act puppet show they had written and produced, having made all the puppets and the stage themselves. The family will go later when David feels better.

Others returning to America this month will be Don and Joyce Harrison, who have worked at Ukpom for the past two years, and Ray and Charlotte Lanham. Ray built the first house on hospital property and has helped with the hospital construction.

The hospital will be ready to open as soon as we can equip it. Donations have been coming in from all over the States and even Europe. One member of the West End Church, Nashville, gave money for the cookstove, and another gave for the washing machine. Dr. Joe Mattox sent a barrel of medical equipment. Women from various churches have sent hospital gowns made from discarded shirts and boxes of rolled bandages from old sheets. Mildred Mattox, Patti Bryant's mother, and her friends collected enough money to buy and ship three barrels of linens. Now the customs officials want to charge us $180 for them, though they are clearly marked "For Hospital Use Only." The government is so self-defeating that even USAID has announced they will be discontinuing their shipments of dried milk to the hospitals because they are being charged customs.

Our visitors were impressed with the amount of Bible teaching at the clinic. Henry has a devotional every morning with the staff before they begin seeing patients. Moses Opara, who fled the North, teaches the construction workers. The registrar, one of our Bible School graduates, has a daily service for the out-patients and gives each one a tract. Some recently baptized by the evangelists told them their baptism was a direct result of the kindness and teaching received at the clinic.

The children have had a dog for about a week now. The pet of a single missionary lady who has died of cancer, the dog has been house-broken and spayed. She appears to be adjusting to kids, but not to the nurses' cats. I've been uneasy about having a dog after the Aba vet told us no rabies vaccine is available.

Lee celebrated his sixth birthday, July 29, with the kids on the compound. Marty made and decorated his cake, and I made ice cream. He received his first model airplane (a new import at Port Harcourt), which he assembled with help from Paul and David.

Nancy Petty and Patti Bryant have been alternating days caring for a newborn whose mother died in childbirth. The father, one of our preachers, is hoping to find a wet nurse. Recently in a similar situation, Nancy had told the father to bring her the baby and a bottle, and she would show his how to care for it. Not understanding the importance, he waited too long. He bought a bottle and some evaporated milk, but he knew nothing about mixing a formula or even that he should wash the bottle. When the man finally returned, the bottle was green inside and caked with soured milk. The nipple was covered with mold and the tip had rotted off. He handed it to Nancy saying, "This one is finished." That baby died of dehydration and diarrhea. Now they are hoping to save this baby.

This is the height of rainy season when it rains for days on end -- sometimes a hard downpour and sometimes an all-day drizzle. Papers, sheets, everything feels damp. Last night we had our first line ant invasion of the season -- of course, after we had turned off the generator. We had to light candles and do the standard procedure -- apply insect repellent, get nets off the floor and bedposts in water to create an island of safety.

In this kind of weather I'm so thankful for a big house and a playporch. The other day it looked as if Lee had dumped out everything he owned. I chided as I helped pick up, "I don't see how on earth you can make such a big mess!" Innocently he answered, "Oh, that's easy, Mama. Picking up is the hard part."

                                        Love,
                                        Dit

Tuesday, August 23, 1966

Dear folks,

    Today we celebrated the formal opening of the first in-patient unit of Nigerian Christian Hospital! The out-patient took a year of red tape and negotiations. Now going into our third year we finally have the in-patient.

    After an opening religious dedication, Dr. Braide, senior medical officer from Aba, cut the ribbon. Local chiefs made speeches each emphasizing his part in bringing the hospital. Dr. Braide, the final speaker, arose and began, "I've heard of lot of talk today, but I've not yet heard anyone say, `Thank you' to Dr. Farrar." Then he went on to say what a privilege it had been for him to have worked with Henry and how impressed he had been with Henry's medical knowledge and personal concern for his patients. I almost felt sorry for the chiefs by the time he'd finished. After all, we must never forget that they did give valuable farmland for the hospital, or it could not have been built.

    The first unit will be the maternity ward, but it will actually be a few more days before Nancy has all the details in place to receive patients -- sterilizing instruments, having more scrub gowns and linens sewn by the tailor, etc. Patients actually arrived today hoping to be admitted.

    I've enjoyed having the best cook on the compound, and now Henry's taking him for the hospital because he says he has to have someone he can trust to be clean and honest. At present Monday John is here during his school break working with Clement, the new steward. Monday learned to cook just watching Tom. The kids are so happy to have Monday "home."

    We signed to be financial responsible for his secondary schooling, but he's worked to pay his expenses all by himself except for

$6. At the same time he has maintained top scholastic status in his class of sixty-seven.

Marty and Paul are both good cooks, but food preparation here is so time consuming. Even a peanut butter sandwich first involves baking the bread from scratch. Then the peanut butter comes after shopping in the market for nuts, roasting them to the right color, rubbing off the inner husks and winnowing them, and finally sending them through the food grinder three times. Winnowing the husks has always been one of the kids' favorite jobs since I go by the old law, "Thou shalt not muzzle the ox when he treadeth out the corn."

For the recent annual women's lectureship at Ukpom, I was assigned the subject of menopause. In the past most of the women died before they reached that age. Now that they are living longer than their mothers, many don't understand what is happening. The women got so excited I had to stop speaking at times and wait for them to be quiet. The interpreter said it was because "they are learning so many new things." I wonder if he said what I was saying, because it was new to him too.

I keep a never-ending pile of papers by my side. Even when I lie down for a siesta, I take a stack of papers and workbooks to bed with me. Besides the kids' school work, I've had two different classes of heath care trainees for which I have to do all the lesson plans and tests. For the missionary kids Sunday School class I try to do something more in-depth than the Bible stories they have heard all their lives. This week I still have a lesson to plan for the ladies fellowship on Saturday.

It would be frustrating if I had not learned to concentrate on being thankful for what I am able to get done, and for what I can't get done I take comfort in a favorite Nigerian saying, "You have tried."

They have taught me so much about living.

Love,
Dit

Tuesday, September 6, 1966

Dear folks,

As I write rain is pouring down so hard our yard looks like a lake -- and we live on a hillside.

On Monday, August 29, six days after our formal opening, the first maternity patients were admitted. We have a registered mid-wife on each shift who is able to deliver any uncomplicated case. Our six beds have stayed full even though patients usually go home the day after delivery. At 5 a.m. the first night after admitting patients we had our first delivery, the wife of our hospital washerman. Henry got up for the occasion, and she was honored with free service, gifts from the nurses, and numerous photos.

That same Monday Iris, as director of nursing education, had a candlelight capping ceremony for her first class of nurse assistants. She has taught them as carefully as if they were going to apply for registration. Wearing uniforms, the students marched into the Bible school chapel singing an Ibo hymn softly. As speaker, Henry talked about the quality of mercy. He has always emphasized (and used as a favorite test question), "Who is the most important person in the hospital? Not the doctor, but the patient." Awards were given for scholastic achievement. Then the girls lit their candles and knelt to receive caps. The ceremony closed with the students repeating the Nightingale pledge in unison. Afterward we entertained them and their families with kola nuts, ground nuts (peanuts), and Pepsis.

In preference over forceps most hospitals here have a machine not used in America -- a kind of suction cup placed on the baby's head inside the birth canal. Then the machine uses a gentle suction which can be regulated by the operator to deliver the baby without injury. Thus it is possible to deliver a baby from a position higher in the birth canal than forceps can allow. Henry used it for the first time a few days ago on a lady who'd had a long labor without progress. He was as happy as a kid with a new toy telling everyone how he "vacuumed' out the baby. Doctors here try to avoid Cesarean sections if possible because they never know whether the woman will have any pre-natal care or even access to a hospital for her next one. She might end up with a ruptured uterus.

Henry continues to preach several times each Sunday. During the past week he also saw over 600 out-patients in the three regular clinic days plus the added pre-natal/well-baby clinic.

The oilmen came back Saturday to work on the well, but this time the bit stuck and they went home frustrated. We have a saying for such, "WAWA (West Africa Wins Again)!"

Six families associated with oil companies now make the one hundred mile round trip as regularly as possible to worship with us on

Sundays. John Blackman from Louisiana has a son, Bobby, Paul's age, who came Friday and stayed until we took him home Sunday night. His dad was called out on the rig and couldn't come for him, so we said, "Don't worry. We'll take you home." To which he replied, "But I don't want to go home." I don't know who is happiest to see another Christian American teen.

Love,
Dit

Sunday p.m., September 25, 1966

Dear folks,

I'm grabbing the typewriter before Henry gets home from playing chess with David Underwood. The kids are enjoying a soccer game in the brief "cool of the day." Sunday nights are the loneliest of the week for me. Writing letters helps me feel connected, like a visit home.

Today Henry preached at a small church on the backroads of Aba. The mud roads were full of deep puddles and the puddles were full of ducks and splashing, naked kids. Henry is teaching Paul to drive when traffic is light, so today Paul drove the whole eleven miles home from Aba.

When Bobby Blackman came today, he brought with him a stack of new LP's, the latest hits fresh from America. With so many oil workers and their families arriving from Louisiana and Texas, ships carrying household goods arrive from Houston non-stop in three weeks. Paul has twice spent the night with Bobby, but it was Marty and Bobby "spinning the platters." Paul retired to his room with a book he'd checked out at the library yesterday.

So many more families are wanting to work in Nigeria than our official "Church of Christ quota" will allow that Rees made another trip to Lagos last week. Immigration is not interested in more missionaries per se. But when Rees was able to point out the progress we'd made in medical and educational fields, they granted ten of the eleven visa requests pending.

Joe and Dorothy Cross have arrived for a third tour. The McCluggage family is already in Enugu. Gid and Ruth Walters are expected to arrive Saturday and plan to live and work in Aba, our first missionaries there. Two single ladies -- Lorraine Cusick, teacher for the missionary children, and Cathy Newberry, a secretary -- hope to be here the following Monday for Ukpom. Dixons and Davidsons are coming soon to work at Ukpom and Ikot Usen respectively. Hazel Buice, a medical laboratory technician, is coming to help us organize that department. Once in the country they are free to teach Bible.

Yesterday my interpreter had three "preaching appointments," as Henry calls them, scheduled for me. We left at 12:30, but by the time we arrived at the last village, about 40 miles away, it was 4 p.m. The market was active, but the church building was empty. The interpreter honked the car horn to announce our arrival. After all the effort I'd put into preparing and coming, my heart sank. "Didn't you say 2 p.m.?" I asked "Why is no one here?" As if it were nothing, he calmed answered, "They'll be here. I said 2, so they would come by 4." So much for "African time." With all eyes on me, I felt I had no privacy to hunt a latrine. At 6:30 p.m. I came home exhausted, appreciative of how the men feel after a day of appointments.

Before Nigeria, I thought African women just dropped a baby like a cow might a calf and go right on farming. What fiction! Now we're wondering if any have a baby without problems. Of course we are seeing mostly those that can't deliver at home. Of the first twelve to deliver in our hospital, three were sections. Many are so severely anemic from malnutrition, hookworms, and malaria they can't afford any blood loss. Others often have deformities from rickets, tuberculosis or osteomyelitis. The heavy head load can cause a swayed back or a tilted pelvis. Our maternity ward stays so full we're planning to open one end of the women's ward that is built, but not fully furnished. Marty herself has sewn two or three sheets a day for it. We've been sending the overflow to other hospitals, the nearest about eleven miles. Tonight a new patient said she'd rather sleep on the floor than go to another hospital, and so she is.

Last Saturday we had our first maternal death. A very anemic young girl who had never been to an ante-natal clinic hemorrhaged after delivery. Her husband brought in six people for direct transfusion, but none were the right type. While he went to find more, she died.

There were no blood banks in the Eastern Region until the Peace Corps began one about a year ago. While waiting for the equipment to start a bank here, Henry has been eyeing these healthy young males in the Bible School as a walking blood bank. But with all their superstitions about blood the question has been how to persuade them to give. Finally he had the equipment and the solution. At his request I walked down to their chapel, and after his talk about the significance of blood in the Bible and the need at the hospital, I lay down on the table in front of the student body.

Henry began, "All of you know this is my wife."

"Yes." came the answer in unison.

"My only wife."

"Yes."

"Do you think I would do anything to hurt her?"

"No."

With that Henry proceeded to draw a pint of my O- blood. There was an absolute hush in the room as all eyes were fixed on me. They watched anxiously as I got up off the table afterward and walked around. I told Henry I would walk uphill to the house and he quickly said, "No, you don't. If anything should happen to you, my experiment is ruined. I'll drive you back."

He promised those who would give blood an orange drink and a can of Nigerian corned beef. That afternoon we had nine volunteers, while others waited to be sure that those who gave did not die or have something bad happen to them. We now have a blood bank in operation, and my pint was the first donation.

Last Sunday Lee bit down on a chicken bone and discovered his first loose tooth. He was so excited that he got his dad's tweezers and, typical of his persistence, worked at it until he had it out. A tooth hasn't yet replaced the one he lost in an accident when he was two, so he really looks comical with one out above and one out below. Without telling me he'd put it under his pillow, he slept on it in vain for two nights. Then he came saying he guessed the tooth fairy was afraid of waking him "cause fairies don't like you to see them." I suggested he try once more, "The third time is a charm." He did and it was.

Paul's looking for something to do now , so I'm going to stop and help him make fudge. In this high humidity, it won't get firm if you don't cut the amount of liquid in the recipe -- another of those tricks to cooking in the tropics that Charla Lawyer taught me.

Love,
Dit

October 9, 1966

Dear folks,

I just thought I was busy before! Now I've added teaching Clement and my kids to be cooks.

October 1 was Republic Day in Nigeria, but the mood was somber. No parades. No school programs. As always we gave our workers a holiday. The people who were so jubilant about the first coup say they see nothing to celebrate. The governor declared it a day of prayer for peace.

We went to Port Harcourt to meet Gid and Ruth Walters and their four year old son arriving that morning. Local markets were open, but European shops closed. A friend who comes to worship with us invited everyone (twenty-five) to the palatial Hotel Presidential for dinner and a dip in the hotel pool. We joked about the Walters' first impressions of Nigeria. Rees said maybe it was better to see that side of Nigeria first. It could give them comfort when they saw the other.

The oil workers in Port Harcourt were forbidden by their companies to leave the city for fear the holiday might bring new tribal conflicts -- and it did. The Northern tribes increased persecution of all "Strangers" (anyone of a tribe from another region) in their midst, not just the Ibos as before.

On Monday, October 3, Nigerian Airways flew hundreds of Easterners back into our region, and then all Eastern airports closed. When the people of Port Harcourt saw what had been done to their people who had held jobs in the North, they began a retaliation against all the Northerners in their midst. Local police had to round up the Northerners for their own protection and ship them by train back to the North. So many were killed that our governor made a plea for all Northerners living in our region to return home because he could not protect them. The Voice of America (VOA) reported on the Port Harcourt riots, so I want to be sure you know we are safe.

I told you earlier about seeing what I thought was Southern Lights at Eastertime. The observatory in South Africa finally answered my inquiry. They wrote that it could not have been because there had been no sunspot activity then, but it was probably an intense airglow in the ionosphere seen at rare intervals in the tropics. Charges build up in the daytime then disintegrate at night, occuring faster in the tropics.

Last week we observed similar vertical lights though not as spectacular.

The kids have switched from tadpole farming their stream catches to snail farming by hunting in the bush or cycling to the village market where snails are sold for food. Like bugs, I never knew there were so many kinds till I came to Africa. Nigeria is home to the largest land snails in the world. David's laid five eggs and now they're all as protective as brooding hens.

David found a harmless rock python and kept it in a box to play with. We didn't have a proper cage for it, and the thing had wanderlust. It was a little disconcerting to open a drawer and find a snake curled up, so I suggested to David that the snake was unhappy and should be free. David didn't seem to mind turning him loose. Perhaps he wasn't eager to hunt live rodents to feed him. Who knows what next!

Love,
Dit

Saturday, November 19, 1966

Dear folks,

We'd just gone to bed when a runner came from the maternity with a nurse's note (An emergency note is never written without a proper greeting first.): "Good evening, doctor. We have a new patient that is bleeding. She has no pulse and no blood pressure. Please come." Since I can't sleep soundly until he returns, I'll use this "bonus time" to squeeze in a letter.

Lee says Nigeria has two seasons -- "wet season and sweat season." You should hear him trying to wrap that one around his tongue with one tooth out above and another out below. The egrets have arrived!

Lagos government is in chaos, Port Harcourt airport reopened, and missionaries come and go. In America David Underwood has checked into a Memphis hospital for tests and from his bed wrote humorous warnings about reverse culture shock. Gaston Tarbet, his replacement, with his wife Jan and eight month old daughter arrived with soldiers swarming the airport, inspecting everything they carried.

Jan said the search seemed to be more from curiosity than security, so she didn't feel too upset when one rammed his hand into a bag of dirty diapers.

Wednesday we are expecting Hazel Buice, the lab technician from New York. We really need her on nights like this when we waste valuable time sending a driver to the village for someone who can type blood.

Bob and Joan Dixon from Delphi, Indiana, arrived October 23, to work at Ukpom. She delivered her fourth two weeks later. They'd even toured Europe en route, three little ones in tow.

Houston and Mabel Ezell with their daughter and son-in-law, Lady Frank and Doug Sanders, are expected Friday to supervise construction at Ukpom for three months. Their arrival is like Santa's.

Before coming to Nigeria, I tried to estimate our children's clothing needs for the next two years. Now that we are almost midway through the third year, I have been surprised how much faster clothes wear out, especially anything with elastic -- maybe because of the tropical sun and frequent washing. It's easy to find material and sew for Marty and me, but not the boys. They don't like the Nigerian style of short pants that our tailor makes. I found a Nigerian-made T-shirt, but every time it was washed it went up in length and out in width. I finally solved the T-shirt problem at the Aba market by digging through the huge bales of used clothing from America alongside the Nigerians till I find some almost new for a few shillings.

Jeans are not sold here. I pass the boys' on down the line as long as they resemble jeans. Myra said she'd seen jeans patched before, but this was a first for her to see the patches patched. I am so thankful that George and Evelyn are willing to shop for us and the Ezells willing to bring things.

We tell everyone to remove labels and pre-wash new clothing so it can be called "used" and if questioned by customs answer "Personal effects" -- or pay. There's a story that a customs official once picked up lingerie from Houston's bag, and he dutifully answered "Personal effects."

We now have a Sears electric wringer-type washing machine shipped from America. Sears rewound the motor for the difference in cycles and we use a transformer for the voltage difference. It's such an improvement that our washerman doesn't mind coming in from the village in the evening when the generator is on.

The Girl Scouts -- Marty and Sara Jo -- planned our Halloween party with a special House of Horrors. Nancy Petty made pawpaw Jack-o-lanterns, and the girls created spooky witches out of raffia. Sara had the prize costume -- a robot made from boxes. I'm always amazed at the ingenuity of these kids when they have so little to work with.

We even celebrated Guy Fawkes Day at the Aba Club on November 5. A British holiday, it's the anniversary of the date Guy Fawkes and fellow conspirators were caught plotting to blow up the Parliament of King James I with gunpowder. After dark British friends built a huge bonfire and tossed on several effigies of Guy Fawkes. Then they shot off fireworks and passed out treats. Rees commented, "Great holiday! Halloween and Fourth-of-July all in one!"

For a small fee we can have country membership at the Aba Club. That gives us a place to eat and go to a restroom when we are in Aba, for the kids to swim, and to see a good movie occasionally. On movie nights the local non-members line the outside of the fence to peek over free and cheer at romantic scenes. Surprising! You often see two male friends holding hands as they walk, but a man would never think of touching his wife in public. Husbands and wives even sit on opposite sides of the building at church. Club membership at Aba also gives us reciprocity with clubs in other cities when we travel.

Now the kids are looking forward to the next holiday, Thanksgiving, and a couple of school days off. Maybe we can even find a turkey in Port Harcourt. A partially ripe pawpaw makes a great ersatz pumpkin pie, and Dottie Beckloff taught me how to make "cranberry sauce" from the seed pods of a local plant.

I'll admit that the incubation period of snail eggs was never previously a parental concern, but when there were no signs of life after David had anxiously hovered over them for weeks, I searched my mind on how best to tell a ten-year-old that they might not hatch. Falteringly I began, "Perhaps they've not been fertilized." Immediately he responded, "Oh, that's no problem, Mama. Snails are hermaphroditic." I had to look it up, but do I have news for him! That may be so, but it still takes two.

Aware that we've not yet had the money to open the new 30-bed hospital ward, Hank and Lee decided to do something about it. They collected and sold seeds. Marty made the packages for them. I learned about it later when they contributed 3 shillings and 9 pence (about 48 cents) -- the children's "mite."

Love,
Dit

December 10, 1966

Dear folks,

This hot (86), humid December evening our family had a tree trimming party -- weatherwise very incongruous. Our foil tree came out of shoe-box storage to be ceremonially dressed with tiny electric lights and as many sparking things as the tiny branches would hold. It's barely big enough to resemble a tree, but we make up the difference by covering the room with kid-art.

Henry managed to get away from the hospital one day last week to take the family Christmas shopping at Kingsway, Port Harcourt. They are always thrilled just to ride the escalator, but this time a little train carried them back into a special grotto to see a black Father Christmas with a long white beard. The kids have been squirreling away shillings for months; so even though we came home at bedtime, they were so excited nothing would do them but to wrap everything that night.

Paul turned fourteen last month -- suddenly taller and leggy, battling pimples. Our family enjoys singing in the car when we travel, but coming home from "P.H." the other night, Marty observed, "Paul can't sing right with us anymore."

I enjoy the holidays so much more here not plagued by all the parties and programs. It's truly family time. I plan a extra week off afterward while my steward is out of school to give the place a thorough spring cleaning. Marty will be moving up a year and starting the eighth grade. School has been so easy for her, she's been doubling her lessons.

We were finally able to open the big 30-bed ward for women and children last week and it's been busier than the maternity. The first patient to be admitted was a little fellow with a protein deficiency who died so soon we didn't even get a photo. The people seem to take it for granted that half their children will not survive (the official statistics) and wait too long to get medical care.

Henry and I went to the Hotel Presidential at Port Harcourt for our anniversary dinner, December 2. The hotel, a plush oasis in that oil-rich city, is the only nice place to eat out, even though it is a 100 mile round trip. We wanted to take in a movie there, but they weren't even sure whether there would be one. The films come by air from Lagos and no one had yet brought one from the airport. So we ended up at home by 9:30. Henry said, "People will think I don't love you coming in at this hour."

We had home-made ice cream for David's birthday without searching Aba for ice. A Bible class sent the Bryants money for a kerosene freezer, and now they can keep the ice on hand.

Tigger is such an important part of the family you'll see him in our Christmas photo, although you can't get the coloring on a blue aerogramme. He's always with one of us. I was sorting laundry from a large round basket in the outside storeroom when I came to bottom, and there was a mouse wildly running in circles looking for a way out. Saying, " Make yourself useful!" I reached up to the clothesline above me, snatched Tigger walking the line like a high-wire artist, and tossed him into the basket. It would be hard to say which flew out of the basket first in terror of the other -- the mouse or the genet. I stood there astonished. Wild genets live on small rodents. Then it occurred to me -- that's one trick only a real mother could teach.

One day after our family was in Aba, one of the kids suddenly remembered having left a window open. They panicked thinking, " Tigger is a big boy now and may decide to explore the world in search of another Tigger." As soon as we were home, they ran through the house calling and searching in vain. As a last effort they ran around the house, and there he was trembling and clinging fearfully to the outer edge of the shutter.

Henry's trying to schedule a trans-Atlantic phone call for your 50th wedding anniversary, December 26. I'll let you know. Thanks for the $5 gift. Checks take so long to clear the banks internationally that our financial status is always in limbo. I'll start with this saving for our next vacation.

Merry Christmas or Happy New year! -- depending on when this arrives.

Love,
Dit

December 26, 1966

Dear folks,

Again, "Happy Fiftieth!" Suddenly Indiana doesn't seem so far from Africa after all! Our three minutes transatlantic went too fast, especially with seven people standing by to say "Hello." Some of the children spoke so softly I wondered if you even heard them. It's surprising you heard anything at all. The call went from Aba to Lagos to the London Exchange, which radioed it to a ship at sea, that relayed it to New York from where they phoned you. The Nigerian lady who did the scheduling in Lagos was as excited as I was because she had been to Indiana.

The call was placed from the new Peace Corps office in Aba. The director, a Texan, worships with us every Sunday. So if you ever need to contact us immediately the best way would be through the Peace Corps. Thanks to them, I am the first missionary here who has been able to a call America from Aba.

I had told Henry that the best Christmas gift would be to call to you on your anniversary -- but $75! How could we afford it! It just happened that a Peace Corps member needed minor surgery so he charged an American price -- a fair exchange. He's been teasing me that for $75 my call consisted of Mom saying, "Is that really you?" And my, "Yes, it's really me." Anyway the important thing was not what was said, but hearing it said. I'm so thankful for parents who can stay happily married fifty years.

"Slim pickins" can't dim Christmas excitement for the kids. Between Kingsway and the SIM bookstore we were able to please everyone. Paul was especially happy with a big book on the oceans and a model of Drake's ship "The Golden Hind" with so many parts it will occupy him for months. Marty liked her watch, diary, collector's doll, and a new dress I smocked from the whipped cream fabric Ezells brought. David was happy with his watch, model plane, and swimming flippers, but he has lived with his favorite gift, Buchsbaum's *Animals without Backbones* (Henry said he'd had one for a college textbook). For Hank and Lee the biggest hit of their books and toys were new plastic animals for their "Animal Land" games (acting out their own stories with animals having the personalities of people).

Nashville visitors brought a looseleaf New Testament with blank spaces for notes that I had requested. Paul and I cut passages out of the Ibo and Effik Bibles and pasted them beside the corresponding English verses to make a tri-lingual Bible. Now Henry can look up the English text then read it in the tribal language. He was really surprised and very happy.

Since first seeing them, I've wanted a dress with the lovely Nigerian machine embroidery. The problem has been that ready-made ones are cut straight up and down the same on both sides, like a doll dress. Unfortunately, I wasn't cut the same way. I finally made my own dress with some well placed darts leaving the sides open so the tailor could turn the dress under the machine and embroider the neck, sleeves, and hem before I finished it. Now it's my favorite dress -- black with white embroidery. For my Christmas Henry found black clip-on earrings to go with it. That may not sound like a "find" there; but every female here has her ears pierced in infancy, and mine are not.

Every few days groups of village children arrive with home-made precussion instruments, like rhythmn bands, and play for pennies -- a seasonal specialty. It does get a little monotonous after listening to the same rhythmn for several minutes, but they enjoy doing it so much I can't help but enjoy their pleasure.

The Harmattan blew in dropping night temperatures to 55 degrees. The Nigerians shiver and wrap themselves in layers of cloth; the kids got out flannel pajamas; I feel energetic; and Henry has asthma.

Love,
Dit

February 2, 1967

Dear folks,

Henry is at the hospital tonight delivering twins by C-section. As people become better educated most twins are being allowed to survive, but there are old traditions that may make some grandmothers feel obligated to discard one or both. In the past anything considered abnormal was believed to be associated with an evil spirit. The practice could even include such minor things as not cutting teeth in the proper order.

We've been living in a dust storm throughout January. Henry needed asthma medicine every day. I don't mind literally "biting the dust" as long as cooler weather comes with it.

Long standing seasonal tribal conflicts have flared up again. Our hospital sits on a hill sloping to a stream with villages of another tribe on the opposite hill. Some on the other hill call themselves Ibibio and some say they are Annamg, but with the two tribes living in such close proximity intermarriage has blurred tribal identities. Whoever they are, all on the other side of the stream understand the Efik language while those on our side speak Igbo or Ibo (the "g" sound blends with the "b"). Usually we just say "the other side."

Historically tribes migrate and streams change course. A section of land near the stream has been claimed by both Ibo and Effik. Since palm oil is the chief source of income here, tempers rise as the palm fruit on the disputed land ripens.

Recently the two tribes lined up on opposite sides of the stream with slings, clubs, machetes, bows and arrows, and home-made muzzleloaders. Rees made several trips to the spot preaching, praying, and persuading them to allow the police to settle their differences. Gaston Tarbet sometimes accompanied him and once Henry went. Finally, the warriors disbanded and returned to their villages.

The Ibo chiefs made a special trip to the hospital to thank the men for their peace-keeping efforts, saying they were sure hundreds of lives had been saved. Henry said it was the first time chiefs had thanked him for anything. He also said that he thought that the men really didn't want to fight but felt an obligation, and so were happy for a face-saving way to go home.

But before all had quieted down, two men going to the clinic along the road in front of our house were murdered. People were so frightened that the usual out-patient load of 200 dropped to 30. Today it is up to 100 as confidence in peace resumes.

Henry has just returned from the hospital saying the total weight of the twins was 14 pounds, and they had been locked together in such a way they could never have delivery normally.

We had hoped to come home for a furlough this summer, but there has been no volunteer to replace Henry. We're now considering a fourth year here. Nor has there been replacement volunteers for the nurses who leave in April after two years' service. The Bryants are returning, and Rees hopes to raise money for the hospital and recruit personnel. The harvest is white. Pray for reapers.

Love,
Dit

February 26, 1967

Dear George, Evelyn, and girls,

Thank you for the boys' new shirts. They looked so neat and proud at church today and were so happy to receive them, they're writing you notes.

Your last letter said visitors from here had reported to West End Church that we needed more money. To clarify our financial situation, I must first explain that it takes so long to transfer funds internationally (sometimes three months) that we try to make sure enough remains in the bank to avoid overdrawing. That alone makes us spend more carefully here.

In the two and a half years we have been here our rapidly growing kids now eat twice as much and the cost of food has doubled. To compensate I have learned more ways to use local foods and how to shop for less from local producers and markets. For instance, Dr. Akpabio's wife raises chickens for poultry and eggs, then grows fresh vegetables using the chicken manure. So I load up cheaper there with one stop. Ours is the largest family here, yet we spend less on food than any of the other families.

With kids who like to climb trees, play soccer, and slide down dirt banks (ant hills), I expect to patch jeans. The clothing problems I described earlier are due more to lack of availability than to finances. I have learned how to buy quality clothing for a few shillings in the Aba used clothing market. For Henry I can buy wash-and-wear cloth in the market and have pants tailor-made for about $10 each.

When we came in 1964, Henry asked for $500/mo. which was adequate. Henry considers himself the most fortunate of all missionaries to have had one church provide all his financial needs. He does not want to seem ungrateful and ask for more. I think I have economized as low as I can go, and the funds still give out before the month's end. We've had to dip into what savings and insurance we have in the States.

Our $500/mo. is budgeted like this: $100 in the USA bank for home obligations, insurance, and emergencies; $50 for church contributions; $180 for food: and $170 for all other expenses. The other expenses include such things as $20 for bottled cooking gas as needed, $5 for kerosene for the fridge and lamps, $40 for household helpers (all these take the place of electricity and utility bills in America). The house has been provided by those who raised the money for building it. That leaves $105 for anti-malarials, clothing, entertainment, gifts, souvenirs, and any other personal expense. We usually take the kids to a movie about once a month for about $5. Our vacations have been financed by gifts from friends.

Petrol (gasoline) runs about 65 cents a gallon, but that and car expenses come from the working fund since most trips are for preaching or the medical work. Also the working fund pays for the children correspondence school because that is an expense we would not have in the States. We are certainly not destitute, but prices do continue to rise here like every other place.

You wouldn't believe how the children have changed in the two and a half years since you saw them. Paul's a lean, lanky teen with a crackly voice. Marty's taller than I, wears a shoe size larger, and worries about a few pimples. Bobby from Port Harcourt, who came for church and enjoyed her company, was sent home during the tribal uprising, but they keep letters flying. David's as sparkling as ever, always chasing bugs, and knows more biology than most college students. Hank could double for Huck Finn with his freckles and fringed raffia hat. He cheers us all by his perpetual smile and kind, even-tempered disposition. Lee's often the proverbial fly in the ointment with his boundless energy and curiosity, but he doesn't intend to be. His white hair and antics fascinate the Nigerians so much, they treat him more like a toy.

The Bryants left last week (22nd), but we are fortunate for the arrival of Windle and Barbara Kee and their children -- Paul (12) and Alicejoy (9). Windle has offered to help Henry with the hospital administration, and Barbara has volunteered for the bookkeeping and secretarial work. Otherwise Henry would have the full load, and as the only doctor, he is often at the hospital several times a night for emergencies. Since I gave up my cook for the hospital kitchen. I have never been busier.

This is Sunday, the loneliest night of the week. I always long for somewhere special to go or something special to do before another busy work week. Our Port Harcourt friends used to brighten our Sundays, and we'd make ice cream after church. Now the political turmoil usually makes them too wary to come. I try to think of something different the kids and I can make for Sunday supper, but even that taxes my resources -- mentally and financially. Writing always transports me home for a visit.

If I don't write tonight, it will be another week before I have time. Even now Marty is getting the younger one settled into bed by playing "soldier" with them so I can write.

Love,
Grace

A letter from Marty to her cousin Betty expresses in her own words how a twelve-year-old faces life on the mission field. As a matter of explanation, bathroom water is stream water, not potable, so it's not used for our teeth.

February 26, 1967

Dear Betty,

We received Paul's shirt the other day. I like it. David wore his to church today with his short white pants. They looked real nice.

Sara Jo is gone. So I don't have anyone to play with.

Oh, by the way, I earned my first 3 cadette badges. Puppeteer, Hostess, and Gameleader are the 3. I now have 30 badges. It sure doesn't seem like it.

I'm working another of those 1000 piece puzzles, only this one has 1007. Pardon me, 1006 because one is missing.

Betty, if you don't want to write to me you don't have to. I know I must bore you. I'm so much younger.

Tonight mother was writing letters, so I had to put Hank and Lee to bed. We were soldiers. First we marched to the bathroom and I (general) ordered Captain Lee to stand at attention till I poured some water for him to brush his teeth with. After Sargent Hank and Captain

Lee had brushed their teeth we marched into the bedroom. I ordered them to sit on their beds and we saluted each other. I ordered them to lie down. Just as I turned off the lights Lieutenant David came in to go to bed. I told the Sargent and the Captain that if Lt. David ordered them to do anything they must do it. I haven't heard a sound from the barracks since. CRASH!!!!! (sigh).

Yours,
Marty

March 5, 1967

Dear folks,

Friday was a fun-filled evening for us all. Six Dutch teachers from the Shell Oil Co. compound at Port Harcourt came for dinner and brought their six guitars. After dinner they played and sang folk songs from around the world for us. Then we all joined in a singing session with them. It reminded me of all the music parties I grew up with in Indiana.

The children really miss their Bryant friends, but at the moment Marty, David, and Paul Kee have a big monopoly game going. Alicejoy has introduced the younger boys to a new game, or more accurately an old one -- playing house. As you might guess she is the mother, Hank the daddy, and Lee left with being the baby.

Since the tribal conflicts have quieted, the hospital beds are full most of the time. There's nothing like making rounds with Henry to cure the blues. Tonight the first patient we came to was an emaciated little fellow who has neither father nor mother, being cared for by an eleven-year-old brother. With treatment for malnutrition and bloody dysentery he is making slow, but steady, progress. The next little boy has been hovering between life and death for days with severe anemia and convulsions from malaria. We think he'll make it now.

Patience, a little girl about nine, has been rightly named. For weeks she's had a plaster cast around her neck that pushes her chin up so high she can't move it. You'd expect her to be unhappy, hot, and miserable; but instead she greets everyone with a big smile because her spinal tuberculosis doesn't hurt her neck anymore. She's been so much fun for the nurses she's become their pet. Now they're teaching her English.

Cornelius, about the same age was next. Another case of spinal tuberculosis, he will be in a body cast for about a year, all the time receiving drugs and injections for his T.B. and vitamins and milk for his malnutrition. The government provides the medicines for the tuberculosis patients. And so it was as we continued down the ward -- every bed having its own story of ignorance, illness, and hope.

At last Henry has his own operating room! No more sending his surgical patients eleven miles to the nearest hospital! With the Kees assuming the administrative and business loads, he is finally free to realize his dream -- practicing medicine and preaching. He's been devoting Sundays to the people of the local warring factions to head off the possibility of a future conflict. I enjoy passing out Bible pictures to patients and playing records I have of Bible stories in their own language.

Henry has always compared Aba with its masses madly dashing about to an ant hill someone had just kicked. Now the population has doubled, maybe tripled. No one know how many Ibos have fled from the Western and Northern Regions in fear for their lives. The surge has brought us several experienced nurses, midwives, and even one anesthetist (trained at a US hospital in Thailand). All happen to be SDA's (Seventh Day Adventists), but hopefully we can teach them too.

Letters describing your heavy snowfall sound like heaven to me just now. Usually late February and early March are the hottest times of the year. In the past we found time to head for the hills, but this year the hospital is full, and Henry has no relief doctor. Even if he did, the political situation has been too precarious. Even our trips to Port Harcourt are now met with road blocks which we'd never had before the political unrest. The first time I heard a soldier say, "We want to examine you boot," I started to pull off my shoes. Then I saw him lift the lid of the car trunk.

Love,
Dit

March 14, 1967

Dear folks,

Iris Hays plans to leave today for Lagos if planes are flying from Port Harcourt. We always write letters when anyone goes to

Lagos. The mail is more likely to get out of the country, and it cuts off about a week of time en route.

She had planned to leave with Nancy Petty and Mike King the end of the month, but she had word through the consulate that her brother stationed with an oil company in Saudi Arabia had emergency surgery, so she's going early to see him. We've always wondered if the emergency notification system could work in Nigeria. It's comforting to know it passed the first test.

Our biggest news, at least as far as the kids are concerned, is that we've added a new family member. Before you get too excited, I'll say, "It's another genet!" A local hunter brought a baby genet to our door Saturday, and it is flourishing under Marty's tender care receiving diluted milk by a medicine dropper. They've named it "Tigre," Spanish for tiger. Because it's a female and Tigger is a male, the kids have vision of supplying all the families with little Tiggers.

Tigger had the free run of the house until we got the dog. Now for his own safety, he's been caged. At the present the two genets hiss at one another. Marty very diplomatically holds the little one near the cage each day until they get acquainted. The hissing upsets her baby.

Henry is in "hog heaven" with his own operating room. Plastic surgery is a special joy because it is such a life-changing procedure and no one else near here does this surgery. The last was repairing a harelip for a young girl. Even though we try to break even on expenses, he did this one gratis because of its value to her life. The most important thing in the future of a Nigerian young lady is her marriageability, and that depends a lot on her appearance. Even Christians have such strong feeling against such facial deformities, they often refuse those afflicted the communion wine -- usually served from one cup. (Grape juice spoils rapidly here without refrigeration.)

Because our hospital is centrally located, the Peace Corps has sent a volunteer to set up a blood bank accessible to other hospitals. Government hospitals with socialized medicine are crowded, and people don't trust government care. Though the average daily wage for hard labor is about 50 cents and most villagers live off the land, they still prefer a native doctor ("witch doctor") or a mission hospital to free government care.

Paul's high school through the University of Nebraska has been the first school work here to challenge him. He works at it mornings, afternoons, nights, and Saturdays -- a good preparation for college -- and usually receives an A or A+.

Paul looks so much like his dad's high school photo, that I tell him, "Paul, if you want to know what you'll look like at forty, turn around." Unlike his dad, he is a person of very few words. One evening Nancy was having dinner with us and Henry, reminding the kids of their manners, said, "Paul, sit up! What woman would want to marry a hunchback." Very softly Paul answered, "Mama did." I thought Nancy was going to choke.

Our American doctor replacements are being drafted as soon as they finish medical school. Our best prospect, Ken Yearwood of Nashville, planning to finish internship next January, has already been called for his physical. He has asked Henry to write his draft board and explain the needs here in hopes of a two-year deferment.

Love,
Dit

5:30 a.m., March 20, 1967

Dear folks,

This is a hurried note by candlelight. Outside it's pitch black dark. Daylight comes on suddenly about 6:00, and that's when I must end. Those who'd already planned to leave Nigeria this year are doing so as soon as convenient while the going is good. We take advantage of every opportunity to get mail out of the country to let you know we are okay and not fearful about our future here. Even Marty's baby, the new genet, is getting fat and glossy.

John and Dottie Beckloff and their family are leaving today after five years of service in Nigeria. They live so far back in the bush (about an hour's drive from here), they've arranged for a taxi to meet them on our campus for an all-day trip to Lagos. There they can arrange travel plans to Europe before returning to Nashville, where John plans to work on a masters at Peabody.

With our first rain in months my corn shot up a foot almost overnight. It's amazing how the whole land can look so brown and dead one day, then suddenly alive and green after one good rain.

The taxi is here.

Love,
Dit

March 26, 1967

Dear folks,

I'm so happy to hear that the Christmas gifts we sent five months ago finally arrived. Postal regulations here make it so difficult to send packages that I'd hate to think all my effort was wasted. First it's hard enough to locate a strong box. Then I must wrap it in heavy paper and finally tie it with cord on all sides plus another knot where every cord crosses. Next I have to melt red sealing wax with a candle and drip it to completely cover each knot. After all of that, I had three boxes ready for three different states. When I requested customs forms, the postal clerk would allowed me only one though they had more! Friday Onyekafor, who does our shopping, says they refuse him as many stamps and aerogrammes as we request. Maybe they're trying to be fair, but it was a Nigerian who complained, "Nigerian civil servants are neither civil nor servants." I had to take it back home and repackage all into one box, which I sent to Evelyn with addresses where to forward each thing inside.

The little package of wood powder you received was originally wood carving from Ikot Ekpene. I learned after I mailed yours that they all have bugs in the wood and must be sprayed to preserve them. So the worms had five months to feast. I can't find anything here that looks like a doll for the doll collectors except small wooden carvings that are used for juju (after a native doctor has gone through the proper rituals to persuade a spirit to live in them). I don't know why they always paint the faces white. Even their memorial statues for the deceased are usually painted with white or blue faces. When I ask why, I get another one of those "because it's our custom, Madam," answers. It seems that every child big enough to walk has another strapped on his back, so why dolls.

After all the hot, dry weather, the rains are as welcome as spring. In fact it feels so much like spring that Mike King, our Hoosier man, say it makes him want to go mushroom hunting. There is an edible local mushroom that comes in season with the rains, but I'd better leave hunting those to the more experienced.

Today was Easter. I boiled five dozen eggs yesterday, but not before I made the kids promise they would eat every one when they were through with their fun (not all the same day). I can't stand waste in a land of so many anemic people. Paul, a natural artist, colored his blue then drew all kinds of ships -- old navy sailing vessels, small sailboats, and a yacht. Taking turns hiding and hunting, they made it a real holiday.

I casually opened one our National Geographics, and there before me was a full page spread with a woodland scene like spring in Indiana. A sudden surge of light-headedness overwhelmed me, and I thought I would faint. I slammed the magazine shut and put it on the bottom of the stack where I would not likely open it again -- and tried to put it out of my mind. I hadn't realized home-sickness could be so physical! When will I be able to kick up leaves or cool my toes in a shady stream!

For several months Nancy Petty has assumed primary care of a motherless child from birth to toddlerhood. Nancy named her Virginia and dressed her in baby frills. Virginia has been a delight to everyone, a real part of our missionary family. Now that Nancy's leave is imminent, she made a decision that so many mothers make when they adopt out their own child. She put what she considered the best interests of the child before her own feelings. She had brought the child through the most vulnerable part of her life physically; and now rather than apply for legal guardianship to take her to America, she gave the child back to relatives to be raised among her own people.

Dr. Spray. on orthopedist with CARE, who had planned to come this spring for three months wrote that he had been advised to cancel his trip because of the present political situation -- another relief doctor gone! The whole nation is like an angry boil coming to a head, and we're all waiting to see when or how it will erupt. The crux will come April 1 when the fiscal year ends. The national government is Muslim controlled, and authorities in the Eastern Region say they will not turn over oil revenues from the wells in their region to those who have persecuted them.

The U.S. Consulate is aware of each American citizen and has plans for evacuation in place if necessary. Our contact man is with the textile mill in Aba. He has been to see us and advised that we keep a month's supply of petrol and canned food on hand in case imports are cut off. Don't worry. Uncle Sam has long arms, and the Lord's are even longer.

Love,
Dit

April 9, 1967

Dear folks,

As expected, on April 1, when oil revenues from the Eastern Region were denied Lagos, the first thing that the Federal Government did was to cut off all flights into the Eastern Region. The Federal Government said their reasons were financial, which may be true since over half their revenue comes from Eastern petroleum. Bill and Mary Lou Curry, from the Bible school in Enugu, left yesterday for America and had to be driven to Benin in the Midwest, the nearest airport with flights to Lagos. Mike King and Nancy Petty left last week shortly before the Port Harcourt airport closed. Charley Bridges, the nurse who had planned to replace Nancy, has been waiting more than a month for a visa.

Henry has not had a day off since we fully completed the hospital. But then we dare not leave this region now. Our friends from Port Harcourt who so faithfully worshiped with us have not come for the past two Sunday. We feel certain that their companies have forbidden them to go anywhere else.

Col. Ojukwu, our Eastern governor, has asked all people from the Eastern Region who are working in other areas of Nigeria to return home. Most have already done so. Their return to an over-crowded, under-employed, mostly rural economy will be a great financial loss to many families. Most had held high-paying positions and were sending money back home. In fact it has been a major complaint from the North that their best jobs were taken by Easterners.

Our thermometer on the political situation has been the Peace Corps, and they still have over 300 here. Over fifty American families are still in Aba with the textile mill, and hundreds are in Port Harcourt mostly associated with the petroleum industry. All of these won't leave until they are forced to shut down.

Since fresh vegetables have been cut off from the North, my garden takes on new importance. I'm harvesting lettuce, green peppers, and greens. My corn is tasseling. my okra blooming, and tomatoes and watermelon coming on.

A fourth year will put a real strain on the boys' clothing situation, especially for David. He wears the same size pants as Paul now (the younger boys can mange with hand-me-downs). Local tailors have no idea what Bermuda shorts are supposed to look like and I can't seem to get it across with catalog pictures. I've tried two tailors and both times I ended up spending hours ripping pants apart and resewing. Barbara Kee brought a pattern book, so I'm going to try ordering patterns from London. If I have to do them myself, I'll do it right the first time.

Our children has been practicing for a track and field day with the missionary children at Ukpom Saturday. With school only half a day and no homework, acres of bush to explore, endless trails to cycle, and a stream to catch fish and tadpoles, the children have never had so much time and space to enjoy. Marty even said, "If it were not for seeing Grandma and Grandpa, I wouldn't ever want to go back to America."

One day David caught an electric catfish in our stream. He knew because it had shocked him when he handled it. He parked it in a basin in the playhouse while he ran to get me to "come and see". When we returned, an opportunistic egret had just downed a fast-food meal.

Love,
Dit

April 16, 1967

Dear folks,

At 10 a.m. it's already 85 degrees, and so humid it feels much hotter. Highs the past few days were above 90. The rains that brought the seeds to life suddenly stopped several days ago, and now the young plants will wither without my watering.

Unless I plant cassava joints or the eyes of yam as the locals do, gardening here is a very tricky business. This sandy loam has long since lost all nutrition to heavy rains and overcultivation. The first step is to pick a site that won't erode and rebuild the soil. Then I have to start seeds in boxes of sterilized soil, or the ants will eat them before they can germinate. Several transplantings later when the plants are finally large enough for the garden, they must be shaded carefully from the blazing sun for a few days. It all sounds like a time-consuming process, and it is. What I began as a diversion and form of exercise is now part of a serious effort to live off the land.

There is talk now of a boat blockade. Shipping lines are required to pay a docking fee before they are allowed to unload. Lagos is expected to require that all fees be paid there so they can be sure of receiving the money, even when the boats would be scheduled for Port Harcourt and other ports in the East. Shipping companies will refuse to pay twice and will probably unload in Lagos. If the imports do make it to us, the price will be considerably higher because of the overland transportation.

So far our airmail letters from overseas arrive as usual, all of which confirms what we always suspected -- they are by air only as far as Lagos. Air transportation to our area is nonexistent. If you suddenly don't receive mail from us, don't worry. We may be blockaded at any time, but none of the American companies here have curtailed their activities.

Well, so much for the weather and politics. The kids had a fun day at the track and field day at Ukpom with the kids of the missionary school there. Lorraine Cussick, the teacher there, organized them into groups by age and emphasized involvement so that everyone received an award. Paul was first in the broad jump, Marty first in high jump and 50-yd. dash, David first in hurdles, Lee first in racing and jumping. He runs and jumps all the time anyway so I guess it finally paid off. Poor Hank was the smallest in his age group, but he tried everything and was happy with his sportsmanship award. Afterward they had a picnic and talked about "next time."

At the hospital the new male ward is ready to floor. Even with the Kees' help, Henry stays very busy, but it's the kind of busyness he enjoys. Most of my time is spent schooling the children. Besides supervising the house work, I teach anatomy for hospital workers, occasionally speak for ladies' church groups, lead our Girl Scout TOFS (Troop on Foreign Soil), and teach the Bible class for our older children on Sunday. Clement has become a capable cook/steward and requires less supervision. Laundry is so easy with an electric machine that I dismissed John, our washerman, in an effort to economize. In a few days he was back asking for a letter to show the village that he had not been dismissed for stealing.

Ibos are very ingenious in devising ways to earn money. He was soon back again proposing that I buy an orange tree from him. It had to be explained to me that this meant I would pay him for all the fruit that one tree produced for the season and he would bring it to me. I had no idea how much fruit a tree should produce. On faith and sympathy I bargained with him. At least it might save time looking for oranges for awhile and help him feed his family. For a few weeks he regularly brought fruit, but later my steward who squeezed the juice told me, "Madam, I could tell that they were not all from the same tree."

John's next offer was to plant me a pineapple garden. I bargained on that one too, thinking I would learn how for the future. I watched carefully as he dug deep holes and filled them with a kind of grass they use for compost before seating the plant. I'm told it takes two years to produce the fruit -- not much help for now.

Nigeria produces the sweetest pineapple and bananas we ever ate, but, true to human nature, our kids long for the unavailable -- apples and grapes.

Love,
Dit

May 1, 1967

Dear folks,

Finally a mini-vacation! Henry found a Nigerian doctor on leave who would relieve him for a couple days while we went to Enugu. Our main purpose was to request one of the doctors who had to leave another region of Nigeria. The government has already placed some in other mission hospitals with government salaries. The load of a hospital, clinics, surgery, and night emergencies is becoming too heavy for one doctor.

While in Enugu we stayed with the Keesees and visited the zoo. The feature attraction was a month-old baby elephant whose mother had been killed while raiding a farm about 100 miles away. Enugu has access to areas of the Eastern Region with a higher elevation where they can produce cattle and a variety of vegetables. Before we returned home, I loaded up with as much beef and as many potatoes and other vegetables as I thought we could use and share before they spoiled. What a difference in our meals since!

While there I lost a gold crown that had been put on by the dental school when Henry was in med school thirteen years ago.

Fortunately, there's a good dentist at the Catholic hospital forty miles away. So our first day back was spent there.

The children had been invited to the Shell Oil Compound near Port Harcourt for the Dutch celebration of Queen Juliana's birthday Thursday. Hank was excited when he learned that her birthday was actually Sunday, the same day as his. The children were divided into groups of about ten according to their ages with a leader for games of skill. Refreshments were candy (unusual kinds they'd never tasted before), cokes, ice cream, and little Dutch dessert pancakes that had been rolled in butter and powdered sugar. Marty placed first in the shooting gallery and had the shortest time for changing a truck tire. For one game she rode a bike under a post and tried to catch a ring with a stick held in one hand. Picking off the ring meant a prize; but if the stick hit the bar holding the ring, it unbalanced a tub of water. She won the soaking. They'll never forget "Queen Julie Andrew's Birthday," as Lee called.

We celebrated Hank's birthday Saturday by taking the kids swimming in Aba then having cake and home-made ice cream at home later. I made a tiered German chocolate cake, and Marty decorated it with a train made from match boxes. We gave him the train board and trains we'd bought from Billy Rees Bryant when they left. Nine years ago I rocked my "sweet Kentucky babe" looking out across the blooming dogwood and wild plums from my hilltop near Harlan -- one spring I will always picture.

We'll keep you informed as much as possible. I've heard that Nigerians are noted more for their palaver than for their desire to fight.

In the meantime, the U.S. Consulate announced that they would be sending no more workers for the Peace Corps or AID to the Eastern Region until the situation calms, but neither would they remove any. And life goes on as usual.

Love,
Dit

May 25, 1967

Dear folks,

Rumors and more rumors! It's hard to know what is really happening. We heard that Gowon, head of the Federal government, had agreed to all the recommendations of the Reconciliation Council last week and that normal communications would be resumed between the East and the rest of Nigeria. Immediately the Ibos demanded secession and began demonstrations.

Henry has had bad asthma the past two weeks along with a sinus infection. The rest of us are well except Lee, who keeps pus on his tonsils in spite of an almost steady diet of antibiotics. The biggest hindrance to removing tonsils here is the lack of good anesthesia; but Henry says, "As soon as we get back to America, that kid's tonsils are coming out." All the specialists we'd consulted before coming vetoed a tonsillectomy. Lee's had problems since his first draining ear at three months, and now we're concerned that his hearing may become damaged.

I helped the Girl Scouts plan a first aid drill Saturday. The other missionary families were here to join us. The younger ones were stationed at different places on the campus with disaster labels such as "fell from a palm tree," "cut with a machete and has large bleeding wound on leg," etc. The older kids had to do appropriate first aid, bring them in and report to the judges. I would never have thought Lee could lie still and be "in shock," but he did and enjoyed it. In fact they all had so much fun they wanted to do it over again, even the victims, and we really had some nice-looking splints and bandages.

We ended with cake and home-made ice cream to celebrate Marty's thirteenth birthday. She received a stack of Sherlock Holmes and Gerald Durrell books, her current favorites.

Next Saturday I will be speaking again for another of the all-day, area-wide ladies' meetings. The day means so much to them, it's a real compliment to be asked.

Our oil drilling friends returned to sink a new bore hole. They gave up on the first. Now we are waiting on a pump and hoping a blockade won't hold it up.

Things have never looked better for us and the hospital or worse for Nigeria. Several people from West End put money in our account there for the children's clothes -- now if I can only find what they need. Nigerians tailors make boys' shorts the British style -- too short and too tight. By the time I rework them with the remnants, Paul says he feels as if he's wearing a patchwork quilt.

Rees' fund raising efforts have been so productive that we should be able to complete the men's ward soon. One Vietnam widow, who wished to remain anonymous, gave $7000 of her insurance for the hospital even though she has children. Ken Yearwood's draft board will defer him at Henry's request. He hopes to come in January along with David Wilbanks, who will also finish his medical training in January.

By the time you receive this we may be living in the newly independent Republic of Biafra. Why "Biafra?" I had to look that one up myself the first time I heard it. Look for the Gulf of Guinea on your map of West Africa, then the little dip on the south side of Eastern Nigeria. That's the Bight of Biafra. It's where we go to splash in the ocean.

Love,
Dit

May 29, 1967

Dear folks,

Just a quick note by someone going to Lagos to make sure you know we are okay. I'm sure the news media there make the situation here sound as sensational as possible, but the political unrest has had very little effect on our lives so far.

I do feel as if I am watching some kind of political chess. Our Eastern Region did vote to secede, but before it could be officially announced, the Federal government preempted and split Nigeria into twelve states abolishing the previous regions. The Eastern Region was divided into three states, and Gowon announced that he would support by force any smaller state that felt threatened by a larger one. No one's saying "Checkmate" yet.

Neither the American nor British Embassies have asked any one to leave. The Embassy is aware of every American here and has an evacuation plan in place if it is needed. More importantly, the Lord is keeping His eye on His own.

Love,
Dit

Evacuation

On Tuesday, May 30, 1967, Governor Odumegwu Ojukwu eloquently proclaimed the former Eastern Region to be "the independent and sovereign state of Biafra" to a wildly jubilant audience. Oxford-educated, a history scholar, he was an admirer of American democracy and patterned his speech after our Declaration of Independence. His speech was so frequently interrupted by cheers that the announcer kept saying the obvious, "The people are cheeeering and cheeeeering!" Enugu Radio broadcast his address in its entirety several times that day. His boast that no nation in black Africa would be able to defeat Biafra was unquestioned.

Every Nigerian around us was just as elated. In amazement I kept asking, "How can you be an independent nation until another has officially recognized you as such? You have no currency, no diplomatic ties -- nothing that sets you apart as a nation but your own statement." With typical Ibo confidence and optimism, they all answered, "Ojukwu will take care of that." I couldn't help wondering if perhaps that's how it was when our own thirteen colonies declared independence.

Immediately the Federal government clamped an economic and communication blockade. While we had continued receiving mail and some goods overland, now even that was cut off. Wednesday was clinic as usual. Thursday we went to the food stores and bank in Aba to prepare for any emergency. I was astonished at how bare the shelves were already. After I had spent $120 on food (all our cash on hand), Henry returned from the bank and said, "Enjoy it. The bank says no more money." We came home with plans to live off the land as long as possible.

With fresh vegetables, peanuts, beans, rice, and beef having been cut off from the North and local poultry farms closing from lack of chicken feed, our basic diet was already mostly fish, white yams, and local greens -- not a bad balance, but limited in ways to prepare them. I could still find some onions and bush eggs to add a little flavor and variety. Basics like flour, sugar, dry milk, and oil (except palm oil) were imports, and I would need to use them very sparingly, not knowing when I might be able to find more.

The American families at Ukpom, listening to ham radio communications among denominations discuss their fears of war and plans to evacuate, made preparations to leave and turn the school over to the Nigerian staff. To our surprise they all showed up at Onicha Ngwa on Sunday en route to Port Harcourt, ready to return to America. Expatriates at Aba had been saying, "Nigerians palaver long, but fight seldom." Besides neither side was really prepared for a war.

Later that day the Embassy-designated contact from Aba Textile Mills came to our compound to tell us that Ambassador Matthews had asked (not ordered) that the women and children evacuate, but that the men remain at their posts. If the situation developed into a war, it would be easier to evacuate only the men, he said.

Monday we drove to Port Harcourt just to see what was really happening. The Hotel Presidential swarmed with evacuees of many nationalities. We found a June 5 edition of the Lagos *Daily Times*. Big bold headlines proclaimed "300 Foreigners Quit the East -- 700 More to Follow." The lead article read: "The first batch of some 1000 foreigners -- including 800 American citizens -- to be evacuated from the three new states carved out of the former Eastern Region flew into Ikeja Airport yesterday. The batch, numbering over 302 wives and children, flew in yesterday in three groups as a Pan African Airlines aircraft made three successive trips between Lagos and Port Harcourt... We understand that yesterday's evacuation was organized by the five oil companies." The families of the oil workers had been ordered by their companies to leave. However Embassy officials said flights would continue throughout the week for any Americans or other expatriates who wished to leave.

We received an "Advice to Evacuees" hand-out which included: "The Embassy will provide transportation, if you wish, from the airport to the USIS auditorium, located at 26 Catholic Mission Street in the center of Lagos and near the Embassy. A reception center has been established in the USIS auditorium in order to assist you in making hotel reservations and onward travel arrangements. The Embassy will do everything possible to assist you in making these arrangements."

Returning to the compound we discussed all eventualities we could think of. I really preferred staying to leaving Henry, taking my chances on what might happen. Now we had no contact with our families in America or the children's school, but Henry's most compelling argument was, "If war does come, I could sneak through the bush or get a boat down the river by myself a lot easier than with a family." Furthermore he could stay a lot longer on the groceries I'd bought to feed a family.

That evening we had a feast. We certainly weren't going to leave the can of ham or strawberries that had been on the shelf for a special occasion to someone else. Our luggage limit for the flight would be 44 pounds each -- and no pets allowed. We didn't pack any household goods because Henry would be there, and we fully expected to return before long.

That evening I tried to think what I valued most just in case we would not return. Photos, of course -- those went in first -- but then what? We told the children to pack clothes, school books to work on until we came back, and whatever they valued most just in case we didn't. Sorry, no genets!

That night lying in bed trying to decide what to take, I realized that the only thing really important to me was our family. We were all well and would be together except for Henry, and the Lord would take care of him. I fell asleep relaxed, determined that this would be my opportunity to show our children that material things were not really that important.

On Tuesday afternoon, June 6, one week from the Biafran declaration of independence, the children and I boarded a plane for Lagos. The Tarbet and Kee families chose to stay at Onicha Ngwa. As the Kees put it, "We just got here. And after all it took to get us here, we are not about to leave now."

Henry had heard of two Christian business men living in Lagos who might be able to help us when we arrived. J.C. Thomas with Gulf Oil had been helpful to missionaries, but we had heard he was home on leave. We'd heard there was a Ted Greer with United Geophysical, but had never met him.

Henry's parting instructions to me were, "Try to contact one of those, and if possible wait in Lagos until this blows over. If you can't, maybe we can meet in Rome. If nothing else works out, you may have to go on to America. Use your own judgement."

With that we kissed good-by. At the doorway to the plane I stopped to look back at a tearful Henry -- both of us wondering when, if ever, we would see each other again.

Lagos

In less than an hour we were being met by Red Cross ladies in crisp uniforms and neat coiffures, who shocked me back into a world I'd forgotten. As we disembarked from the airport bus, a form to be processed by the Embassy accompanied the coffee and doughnuts.

The USIS auditorium was filled with a crowd making its way to a line of tables across the front where clerks were assisting each group to its destination. I scanned my paper.

"Name ___ " I knew that.

"Sponsor ___ " Another score -- West End church of Christ.

"Travel plans ___ " Locating a phone book, I decided to try United Geophysical. The phone didn't work.

I watched others, group by group, being whisked off to the Federal Palace, the most luxurious hotel in Lagos, in big, black company limousines. The next day a special Pan-Am flight from America would come for them, and they would be with loved ones.

In a land without twilight, darkness was coming fast. The room was almost empty. Repeated efforts to use the phone had failed. It was suppertime and I had no money. I hadn't the faintest idea where I would spend the night. A city of a million people surrounded me -- and I didn't know one. Five hungry children were looking to me for answers. Loneliness swept over me. How comforting it must be to rest in the long arms of some oil company and hear, "You belong to us. We will take care of you. Tomorrow you will be at home in America."

Suddenly it dawned on me. What was I thinking! I work for the One who owns all the oil. When the next kid asked, "Mama, what are we going to do now?" I was ready. Picturing Moses beside the Red Sea, I answered. "Wait! And you will see what the Lord has in store for us."

It was completely dark outside, and I was alone now in that huge hall with only my brood and the clerks. I handed one my paper, almost blank. He looked puzzled at the empty lines and back up at me, "What are your plans?"

I couldn't let him know I had no idea. With fresh bravery, I replied, "I won't know until I contact this man," and gave him Ted Greer's number, wondering all the time if such a person really existed. "The phones don't work," I added. " I've tried all afternoon."

He shot up the antenna of a walkie-talkie, "Get me Ted Greer with United Physical." I'd forgotten American technology!

I held my breath.

In a instant, a voice answered, "This is Ted Greer. What can I do for you?"

"There's a woman here with five children who came in from the East today and says she is to contact you."

My "heart was in my throat." What would he say to that!

I could hardly believe what I was hearing. "Tell her to wait right there. I'll be down in a few minutes."

Soon there was our big, black limo! Introducing himself, Ted surprised me with, "We've been expecting you." Expecting me? He continued, "We know about all the trouble in the East, and we knew the missionaries would be coming through soon."

At his apartment we met his wife, Ada, and their two sons, Eric and Kendrick. No one could have made us feel more at home. While she cooked dinner, both families were making the most of having new American friends.

J.C. Thomas had left the key to his apartment with the Greers for any missionary who needed a place to stay. Better than Federal Palace was the beautiful, large, air-conditioned apartment over-looking the bay in an exclusive neighborhood leased by Gulf Oil for their executives. Ada would come in the morning to take me shopping for food, she said.

Lagos was edgy and soldiers were everywhere. Returning from shopping the next morning, we hit a road block. Examining my passport, the soldier demanded gruffly, "Do you know your visa has expired?"

"Yes, sir."

"Do you know you are in this country illegally?"

"Yes, sir."

" Why has this not been renewed?"

"I have just arrived from the East. We were blockaded. I had no way to renew it."

The officer stomped and stormed, "Do you know I could have you arrested and deported?"

Finally Ada said, "Officer, five children are waiting at an apartment for her to bring food. If you will tell us what you want us to do, we'll be glad to do it."

"Do! If you were a man, I'd know what to do with you! But what can you do with a woman and five kids!" And with that he let us go.

Out of his sight I turned to Ada, "He didn't even notice that the passport itself had expired."

Safe at the apartment, Ada said, "Give me your passport. Ted has a man working with the Embassy who can take care of your passport and visa. Don't leave this house until I bring it back."

Waiting and Leaving

Lagos gave me access to the world outside Nigeria. When the word spread that I was there, help and encouragement came from unexpected calls, visits, and letters.

Jim Massey had deposited money in a Lagos bank for his future visits and wired the bank to make it available to me. Leslie Diestelkamp, a missionary in the Lagos area who had hosted Henry during his 1963 exploratory visit, came to see us several times to offer his services. Ed Enzor, our travel agent, was in town on business and had Sunday lunch with us at the apartment. Paul Dillingham, working in Freetown, cabled "Room for you in our hearts and homes," in case I should want to wait there. I could not name all I heard from.

The Greers took us to church on Sundays and grocery shopping. Eric, 14, and Kenrick, 11, were ideal playmates for our kids. Together they went swimming at the club, played croquet and badminton, and watched TV. By public transport we visited the museum of African art and antiquities and were even able to take a ferry to the ocean beach. Paul had packed his spyglass and enjoyed watching the ocean vessels from our balcony. And there was the school work.

In a few days Henry and I had worked out our own postal system. The Peace Corps, Aba Textiles, and other businesses were still operating in the East and had blockade runners.

Occasional saboteurs kept soldiers busy. Sometimes they would empty a bus we were on, then allow the passengers back on one by one as they checked papers. One day a bridge was blown up shortly after Ada and I had crossed it returning with groceries. One night our whole building shook. I learned the next day that a bomb had gone off at a nearby police station. I would remind the kids of Puddleglum in C.S. Lewis' *Chronicles of Narnia*, their favorite books, saying it didn't matter whether we were here or there all was "in Aşlan's paws". For more than a month more turmoil was happening in Lagos than in the East.

On June 30, as I was reading aloud a letter from Henry saying he would be in Lagos that week-end, I stopped to exclaim, "He can't do that! Troops are lined up now on both sides of the Niger." Paul, who had been looking out the window, said calmly, "Mama, a taxi just drove up, and Daddy is getting out."

Since we had left Onicha Ngwa, everything had continued there as usual. Henry had been seeing about 200 out-patients three times a week plus about 100 for maternity clinic. He'd averaged around ten major operations a week, and opened the new men's ward increasing hospital beds to fifty. So far he had not been able to find a refugee doctor to help. Having had no vacation for more than a year, he closed the hospital for two weeks and came to be with us, to rest, and to re-evaluate the situation. He'd had no problem going through the blockade and, in fact, said hundreds were passing through daily.

We had been expecting a climax in July when Shell British Petroleum would owe Nigeria about $2 billion for drilling rights. Who would receive it? If they paid the Federal Government, the East would not allow them to operate. If they paid Biafra, the Federal government would take action. When the deadline came, they gave a partial payment to Biafra saying that though they regarded them as a rebel regime, they did have de facto control of the oil fields.

Immediately the Federal government announced a march on Enugu, the Biafran capital, several hundred miles north of our hospital. By July 6 skirmishes were reported by radio without major gains from either side.

A letter from Henry's mother informed us that Evelyn, George's wife, had fallen in the rain as she left church the previous Sunday, June 25, and had broken her hip. On July 10 we received a telegram from Henry's brother George that their mother had fallen and broken her hip. With Evelyn disabled there was no one to look after her. Our plans were being revised day by day.

If all was still quiet near Aba, perhaps we might even return, and pack household goods for storage while Henry found a doctor for the hospital. Then we could go to America together. We went by the Embassy for an update on the situation in the East and learned that we knew more than they did. I joked that I might become the only one to be evacuated twice.

Fighting had escalated. In the end, we decided that Henry alone would return to Onicha Ngwa, pack our things, find a doctor to take the hospital and a lawyer to draw up a contract with him. Henry helped us move into a Lagos hotel, though Brother Thomas had insisted we continue at his apartment after his return the 15th. Henry withdrew money to take to Onicha Ngwa for himself and the others there and left July 13 to return to Onicha Ngwa.

The following day the children and I were at the Federal Palace returning from a trip to the beach when we were surprised to see members of the Peace Corps we had known in the East. About 125 Corpsmen had been working in that region, and I knew that they would be among the last to go. They told us they had just arrived, and as of that day Ambassador Matthews had said all Americans must leave. He was not making a public announcement, but evacuating them in small groups rather than a mass exodus.

Rainy season had kept us confined to the small hotel room on most days. The kids were tired of books and games. I told them, "Daddy will be along soon. We are taking the next plane to Rome." The next day we were at the Alitalia office.

I was unaware that the West End church office closed on Fridays. Phone calls from Alitalia were unanswered. Without any assurance that the church would pay for tickets other than my word, I convinced the Alitala office to issue me six tickets to America with a stop-over in Rome leaving Lagos on Monday, their next flight.

I sent a cable to Keith Robinson requesting him to make hotel reservations. I phoned the Embassy, "My husband will be coming through shortly and will want to know where I am," and gave them Keith's address. Greers would be leaving for Rome the following Friday, and we exchanged the names of contacts.

At 11 p.m., Monday, July 17, the children and I said good-by to Nigeria.

Henry's Exodus

With the cash inside his Bible and a supply of tracts, malaria medicine, and aspirin, Henry headed east knowing he'd be interrogated and frisked at army road blocks. Once when asked his business, he said, "Missionary," and alarmed soldiers who mistook it for "Mercenary." Thereafter he stuck to, "Doctor," and reminded them of General Gowon's promise that the army would not hinder hospitals. At each stop he was asked his destination, and he'd name the next town, not his final one. Leaving Lagos he answered, "Benin." At Benin he said, "Asaba." On the western side of the Niger he was able to hire someone to ferry him across into Biafra.

He said he couldn't count the number of times his socks were checked, but no one ever looked in his Bible. David Underwood later said, "That's good. Where your money is, there will your heart be also." When the soldiers picked up the Bible or seemed uncertain about him, he immediately began distributing tracts and dispensing medicines with instructions and was allowed to pass.

He was scarcely back at Onicha Ngwa before the Embassy asked all Americans to leave. Lavera and Eno Otoyo had decided to stay at Ukpom. Henry went there to tell them that the expatriates at Onicha Ngwa were preparing to go and took our most prized possessions for them to care for -- the genets, the washing machine, our large painting of an African buffalo and the big speaker for the record player with our collection of "LP's".

Later the Otoyos came to Onicha Ngwa prepared to help the families pack and transport everything to Ukpom for storage. By then word had gone out to the villages that the missionaries were leaving. While the Otoyos were there, a large group local citizens converged on the compound with war paint and homemade weaponry of all kinds.

There was so much confusion that Henry said he was never certain of their intent. Were they worried that the hospital would be given to someone outside the local communities who would seize the farmland they had signed over? Did they see this as their opportunity to take control of the hospital? Did they hope to keep the families from leaving and maintain status quo?

Fearful for the Otyos, Henry told them to leave immediately without taking anything, stop by the Nwaigwe police station on the opposite hill, and send the police. When the police arrived, they took one look at the angry mob with all the paint and paraphernalia, and they paled. Henry described them by saying he was joined by two more "white" men. (After the war we were told that one of the mob had been assigned to kill Henry and another to kill Friday.) The police managed to calm the crowd enough to convince them that they had to let the missionaries leave.

Brother Akandu was given the keys to the houses, and Moses Opara was left in charge of the hospital and to secure a doctor. There was no time to do anything more than to go while they could with police assistance -- papers left on the desks, food in the refrigerators. The dog would have to find his own food or be food. They left the cars behind locked gates at the Aba Textile Mill as they departed for Port Harcourt.

After the war we learned that the Otoyos had been able to return later and pack everything in metal drums, but they dared not remove anything from the compound. The genets, deprived of the only family they knew, had refused to eat and pined away.

In Port Harcourt, John Freeman, who owned a drilling supply firm, took care of the families until the Italian freighter that would take them to Lagos was ready to leave port. He gave Henry his personal American Express card to use as needed and blankets to keep them warm on the boat. For breakfast on board Henry bought crackers and cheese, and instant coffee with a metal cup and candles to heat the water.

The freighter, made to carry only a few passengers, was packed with several hundred evacuees. The women and children were sheltered below deck while the men stayed above in drenching rain.

It was Thursday, July 20, when Henry arrived in Lagos harbor after a wet night on deck. The Kees and Tarbets had decided to go to the Camerouns. Before disembarking, Henry phoned the American Embassy to locate us and was told that they knew nothing about us. He later said, "Some men don't know whether their wives have gone to the grocery or hairdressers. I didn't know which continent mine was on!" Had we stayed in Africa, gone to Europe, or to America?

He was able to phone the Greers who told him, "She's in Rome. We're leaving now for the airport to go tonight. See if you can get on the same flight."

Henry refused to take, "No seats," for an answer, and in the end his ability to insist and persist won him a ticket.

Rome and Home

"This must have been how the Garden of Eden smelled!" I thought. An overwhelming aroma of fresh fruit filled the air as the airport bus entered Rome. Apples, peaches, grapes -- an abundance of all the fruits I'd missed for three years!

I had phoned Keith Robinson, who was to be our contact, from the airport, so we had no problem finding Pensione Fiorenteni, where he had made our reservations, only one block from Central Terminal Station in Rome. Later he came by to see if all was satisfactory, then left Italy for the annual retreat of the European missionaries.

Two missionary interns, Dee Bost and Jan (now Mrs. John Fortner) helped us find our way around the city. I apologized for imposing on their time, but they insisted that "since all roads lead to Rome," their duty was to help visitors so that the full-time missionaries could get their work done. First I needed money. Dee and Jan took us to the American Express office where, without my having ever owned a card, I persuaded them to give me the cash I needed for Rome.

The pensione owner spoke English and was very helpful. He didn't hesitate to let us know his biggest problem with Americans had been their running water in the shower until his tank was dry. "We believe in being clean," he said "but not wasteful!" The shower and toilets were down the hall, but the room did have a lavatory and a toilet -like appliance that was new to me. I didn't dare ask it's purpose, but we soon discovered it was good for hot, dusty feet at the end of a long sight-seeing day.

Paul had enjoyed Roman history and was eager to see the ruins. Rome is full of drinking fountains, and in that dry Mediterranean air we tanked up at every one. After three years in Africa where humidity is high and drinking water an effort to produce, Marty would say, "I feel guilty drinking so much water." Just watching traffic weave in and out with no marked lanes and no accidents was fun for us, but even better for the younger ones was the pedestrian right-of-way. They kept wanting to cross the streets just for the fun of bringing traffic to a halt.

Saturday morning, July 21, I phoned the Greers at their hotel as we had planned. The first thing Ted said was, "Have you seen your husband? He came in with us last night."

I knew his first attempt to reach us would be to phone Keith -- but Keith was in Germany. As soon as possible, I phoned the girl who had a key to Keith's house and asked if she could go there and wait for Henry's call. Next I sent Paul and Marty to the terminal to watch for Henry. In that huge central terminal teeming with thousands of train and bus passengers going to all parts of Europe, finding one person would be like looking for a "needle in a haystack." Meanwhile I waited by the phone at the pensione.

Henry told me later that when he had received no answer to his call, he presumed he did not really know how to use Italian phones. He then took a taxi to Robinson's house. The driver gave what he presumed was a running commentary on all the sights, but all Henry understood was the frequent interjections of "la bella Roma."

Finding no one at home, Henry returned to the terminal area and checked into the YMCA. There he asked the clerk to try Keith's number for him. By that time the girl with the key had arrived and told him where we were -- only a few blocks away. As he was walking to our pensione, he and the kids spotted each other. In less than four hours and in a city of two and a half million, the Lord had brought our family together again.

During the next few days of sight-seeing, when we could get Henry past the iced watermelon stands, we tried to contact his brother George to learn the situation in Nashville, but got no response. Our original plans had been to take an European vacation with the family at the end of the tour, but Henry said, " I can't enjoy running around over Europe not knowing how my mother is doing," and we'd had no word since we'd been inform of her hip fracture. George told us later he had sent a telegram (which we never received) telling us to take our vacation as planned.

On July 26, 1967, exactly three years from the day we had arrived in Nigeria, we arrived back in Nashville.

Jet-lag and reverse culture shock (though it had not yet been named) had me in a daze, but more imperative than rest were other needs. Henry was shopping for a car, while I was thinking, "In three days our family will be introduced to the West End congregation, and I don't want them looking as if they'd been clothed out of a `missionary barrel' -- first stop Sears."

The helpful clerk at children's wear asked, "What are you looking for?"

I felt so foolish, but how else could I say, "I don't know. What are kids wearing now?"

When the check-out clerk asked to see my driver's license as an ID, I surprised her with, "Will a passport do?"

As I left, I heard, "Thank you for shopping Sears." It echoed in my mind all the way home. No more haggling for that last price. No more leaving with a purchase wondering if I should have offered more or did I give too much. When was the last time I'd heard someone say, "Thank you" for shopping?

Sunday came and we were ready. Only Jim Bill McInteer could have thought to conclude our introduction with, "We've been trying for months to get Henry to come home and rest, but it took the Lord two broken hips and a war to get him here."

Epilogue

Dr. Farrar returned as soon as possible after the Biafran War and found that the hospital's buildings had been completely looted but not demolished. By 1971, families were allowed back into the area, and Grace returned with the four younger children, leaving Paul and Martha enrolled in Harding College. They served at the hospital helping reactivate it to full operation. Today the hospital is a 100 bed facility accredited by the state for training physicians and midwives. The Farrars continued to make annual tours with medical teams.

While our children were together in Nigeria playing in the stream, climbing trees, and riding their bikes free from negative social pressures, fellow missionary Patti Bryant commented, "Aren't you glad our children can have a normal childhood?" As adults, the Farrar children have all expressed appreciation for their overseas experience. As one of them said, "The best thing my parents ever did for me was to demonstrate their faith by leaving the comforts and security of home to launch into the unknown for the Lord."

Nigerian Christian Hospital (1967)

ADDENDUM

Helpful Hints for Living in Nigeria
(As it was 1964-67)

Substitutes in cooking:
Semolina used like cornmeal can make good cornbread.
Green plantain sliced thin, fried in deep fat makes good
     chips. Ripe plantain can be roasted or candied as you might
     sweet potato.
White yam can be prepared as potato. To fry, parboil first
     until barely soft.
Sliced green mango makes good apple pie; the ripe ones are
     like peach pie.
Paw-paw, not too ripe, can be used like pumpkin, can be
     cooked like a vegetable, or used as a meat tenderizer.
Corn-on-the-cob hard enough to shell can be made into
     hominy by boiling it with soda till soft and the husks can
     be rinsed off.
Egusi ("melon") seeds make a good meat substitute. Readily
     available in the markets, they should be rinsed. Then pick
     out any hulls and trash and grind to use like ground beef.
     Roasted until golden and salted, they are ideal snacks.
Water leaf, wild greens growing profusely, is almost like
     spinach.

Cooking Hints:
    Store market beans in metal. I had bugs hatch out and make my Tupperware look like a sieve. Soaking before cooking brings out the bugs. Pour them off with the water, then cook as usual.
    It's worth the extra to buy better quality market rice. Otherwise you may find yourself going through it, grain by grain, to remove tiny bits of rock that looks like broken grains -- or chip a tooth.
    Test bush eggs. One way is to hold them to the light between your index finger and thumb, shading the egg with your hand. If dark, beware! Another way is to put them in a pan of water. An older egg will have a larger air bubble inside and upend.
    Don't be alarmed about weevils in flour or rice. A scrap of mosquito netting makes a good sifter to remove them from flour. Rinse the rice, and you won't know the difference.
    If you don't have a knife sharpener around, try your concrete step.

Water inside a green coconut is delicious, but don't try to cook with the meat of it. When buying a coconut check for cracks that may have caused it to spoil and shake it to listen for water inside. To use fresh grated coconut for American recipes, dry it out first in the oven or sun, or else cut back on the amount of liquid in the recipe.

Baking powder in the shops is not "double acting" as in America. Do your own doubling. If you can't find baking soda in the food stores, try the "chemist" (pharmacy) and ask for soda bicarbonate.

Peanut oil is best for frying, but an entrepreneur may have diluted what is labeled as such with a less expensive oil. Palm oil lends its own distinct flavor and is high in cholesterol.

Sugar can always be found in lumps and cubes (used mostly for tea) or a granulated form called castor. Demerara sugar is like brown sugar and treacle like dark molasses and can be used as such.

Learn British terms. Food comes in "tins" not cans, and don't leave tomato paste or acid foods in them after opening. They're not lined. Flavorings are called "essences." Ground beef is labeled "minced beef." Peanuts are "ground nuts." "Salad cream" is not our salad dressing. Gelatin desserts are "jellies."

The popular Bird's Custard Pudding Mix will taste more like our instant mix with the addition of more sugar and a little butter and vanilla.

Use American measuring cups and spoons for American recipes. There is a difference from the British ones available in shops.

Dry cereals, crackers, etc. are usually limp unless packaged in metal, but crisp up well in a slow oven. Watch carefully to prevent scorching!

Fresh pineapple contains a lot of liquid. Adjust recipes accordingly. Don't try to use the fresh in jello.

Fudge, 7-minute icing, etc. must have the amount of liquid called for reduced or they will be too soft because of the high humidity.

An extra precaution: Drugs bought in the market should be carefully checked. Henry tasted an antimalarial he bought there and knew it was a fake because it lacked the bitter taste. Be sure any bottled water you buy comes with a tight unbroken seal. Sometimes they are refills.

Favorite Nigerian Snacks

Since most Nigerian homes did not have ovens, snacks food were usually fried or roasted over charcoal or in ashes, Their favorite oil is the local palm oil that imparts its own taste and is high in cholesterol. Peanut oil is preferable for frying. It can be heated to a higher temperature without smoking so that not as much is absorbed, and it can be used over again.

Akara (Fried bean balls)

Soak white beans long enough to remove skins -- usually overnight. Grind until smooth. (most electric blenders can do a good job with the addition of a little water.) Beat with a wooden spoon to incorporate air.

To each cup of ground beans add about 1/2 small onion chopped fine and 1/2 teaspoon salt. Mix well with fork. Slowly add water, stirring well after each addition, until the batter will drop fairly easily from a spoon. Hot pepper or Tabasco may be added to the batter to taste. Drop by spoonful into very hot frying oil. If too much water is added balls will spread out into the oil and not form balls. If too little is used, or balls too large, they will cook on the outside before they are well done in the center. Drain well. Serve hot.

Akara eggs: Fold thick akara dough around shelled hard boiled eggs. Use a slotted spoon to lower gently into deep hot oil and to remove. Drain on paper towel or brown paper.

Plantain Chips

Slice green plantain (or green bananas) into thin slices crosswise. Fry quickly in hot oil. Drain well. Keeps well in air tight container.

Roasted Egusi

Egusi is the inner kernel of the seed of a small native pumpkin (often called "melon seed"). It is bought by the cupful in the market. Pick out any outer shell or trash and wash, then pat dry with a towel. Spread thinly on a cookie sheet and roast at a low oven temperature, stirring frequently so they do not burn. Watch carefully after you hear the first pop. Roast to a golden brown. Moisture inside the egusi seed makes them swell and pop. Remove and sprinkle with salt. Cool and store in an airtight container.

Fried Meat Pies

For each cup of flour add;
1/2 teaspoon baking powder
1/4 teaspoon salt
Cut in 1 tablespoon shortening

Beat egg with 1 Tablespoon water and add just enough to make a stiff, but rollable dough. Roll fairly thin and cut into round using a small saucer. Fill 1/2 side with your favorite cooked meat and vegetable mixture. Dampen edges and fold other half on top. Press edges tightly together. Fry in deep fat.

Note: Beef cooked with chopped potato, carrot, onion, and garlic is a favorite, but if too soupy it will leak. Another variation is sausage balls inside the pastry.

Scotch Eggs

Hard boil 6 eggs, cool, and shell. Cover each completely with sausage (takes about 1 lb.).

Beat egg with 2 Tablespoons milk and dip the covered eggs into this mix. Roll in bread crumbs. Fry in deep fat until golden brown (about 5 min.). Drain and serve.

Family Favorites from Tom Ibe

Ground Nut (Peanut) Stew

Cover stewing chicken (2 1/2 to 3 lbs.) with water.
Add: 1 teaspoon salt or chicken bouillon cube (Maggi cube in Nigeria)
1/4 teaspoon hot red pepper
1 medium sized onion chopped fine
1 or 2 cloves garlic chopped fine

Bring to a boil, then simmer until meat falls off bone.
Remove chicken from soup and debone.
Measure 1/2 cup natural peanut butter per lb. of uncooked chicken into a bowl and mix in broth until smooth and thin enough to return to pot. Return meat to pot and cook on low heat for at least half

an hour. (In America I use a crock pot and leave it on low until ready to serve.) Vary according to taste with more peanut butter or bouillon.

This makes a sauce to serve over hot rice with side dishes of fresh fruits and vegetables to be served on top or beside stew. Taste and add more salt or pepper if preferred. The peanut butter thickens the stew, but if it seems too thin add a little cornstarch that has been dissolved in a little cold water first. Stew thickens as it cools.

Side dishes suggested: chopped tomatoes, chopped raw onions, orange sections, chopped papaya ("paw-paw"), grated coconut (fresh or toasted), chopped bananas (add a little orange or lemon juice to prevent darkening before serving), chopped peanuts.
Nigerians usually sprinkle more ground hot pepper on top.

Ube and Egg Sandwiches

If you enjoy egg and olive, this hits the spot.

Have water boiling and drop in ripe ube for exactly 1 minute. Any longer bring out a bitter taste from the seed. Remove the peel and remove the green meat from the seed. Add chopped hard boiled egg, salad dressing, and salt to the green meat as desired for a sandwich filling.

Fluted Pumpkin Leaf Greens

Wash and removed any hard stems. Chop leaves fine and cook in water with a little salt until tender. Drain. Fry chopped onion and a little garlic. Add greens to pan with onion and stir in beaten egg. Stir until egg is set. Good seasoned with bacon.

Fluted pumpkin is a large fluted long green pumpkin grown in Nigeria for the edible seeds and leaves. The cooked leaves taste much like our turnip greens.

The Lawyer Legacy

It has been said that no one truly understands a culture until they understand its sense of humor. Doug Lawyer captured it. Few people understood the Nigerians the way he did, and no one was ever more loved by those with whom he associated -- both Nigerian and expatriate. He put his heart into every phase of his work, yet he always had time to laugh and joke.

He was always trying to make the lives of the missionaries more comfortable and the campus more beautiful. Two full time yardmen went around tending the grounds and filling in sunken places. Visitors always commented on our beautiful lawn, shrubbery, and flowers. He experimented with growing vegetables, and I profited from his suggestions and his boxes of tin cans with the ends removed to protect seedlings. He did not allow chickens on campus. Not only do they attract flies, but Nigerian free range roosters never understood there was a Scriptural time for cock-crowing. They announced their presence at any time day or night, and their favorite location seemed to be under a bedroom window. He also had the palm fronds with weaver bird nests cut back to keep the birds on the move and their noise away from the houses.

Doug had his own way of dealing with personnel problems. He would awaken at unpredictable hours during the night and shine his "torch" (flashlight) across the campus. If the "watch night" did not beam back, Doug went to see where he was. If he found one asleep, Doug would bring his sandals and light back to the house with him. An embarrassed watch night would have to claim them in the morning. Too much of that could cost the job. Disciplinary action for a student often involved some kind of labor -- sometimes digging out the root of a palm tree stump. It is unbelievable what a large root base one can have. No one would want a repeat on that.

No one enjoyed sports and social activities more. He was responsible for our tennis court, barbecue pit, and concrete picnic table. He promoted student tennis and soccer matches.

He had raised the funds to construct the house in which we lived, then he and Charla moved into a smaller one when we arrived. He and Rees Bryant worked untiringly to secure the land on which the hospital was built. Without their effort there might never have been a hospital in that location.

Like Will Rogers, I don't think Doug ever met a man he didn't like with perhaps one exception. He told me once that when he looked into the eyes of some of the old pagans, he felt as if he were looking into the eyes of Satan himself. His interest in preaching the gospel in Nigeria extended to every contact from the oil workers to the mud huts and continued throughout his life. He made several return trips to Nigeria and served on the African Christian Hospital Board until his death.

Both he and Charla put a great deal of effort into training efficient workers for future missionaries and for the workers' job security. Doug taught Friday Onukafor to drive. When the Lawyers left, Friday was invaluable as a driver by freeing missionaries from many tedious time-consuming tasks. Charla taught Friday to cook and Mark Appollos, who served as his apprentice, has been an excellent cook for Americans since. Most of Mark's recipes were Charla's.

I never hesitated to go to Charla for any problem I had -- cooking, shopping, personnel, etc. She was always eager to help. I respected her courage for being the first of our missionaries to have a baby born in a Nigerian hospital.

Visiting missionaries have reported that one of those about whom Nigerians most frequently inquired have been the Lawyers. There will always be a special place of honor for the Lawyer family in the memories of Onicha Ngwa.